An
Illustrated Dictionary
of Classical Mythology

Gilbert Meadows

An
Illustrated Dictionary
of Classical Mythology

BLOOMSBURY BOOKS
LONDON

First published in 1978 by
JUPITER BOOKS (LONDON) LIMITED
167 Hermitage Road, London N4 1LZ.

This edition published 1988 by
Bloomsbury Books an imprint of
Godfrey Cave Associates Limited
42 Bloomsbury Street, London WC1B 3QJ
under license from Minotaur Publishing Co Ltd

ISBN 1 870630 60 2

Printed in Yugoslavia

Philosophy can bake us no bread,
but she can give us God, freedom
and immortality.

NOVALIS

A

ABACUS 1. Flat stone surmounting an architectural column, taking the weight of the building. 2. Dice board. 3. Counting-table drawn on sand. 4. Counting-frame.

ABARIS A priest of Apollo who lived without food and rode on a golden arrow given by the god.

ABAS 1. A son of Celeus, king of Eleusis, who mocked the visiting earth-goddess Demeter for the avidity with which she drank a whole pitcher of barley-water, and was instantly changed into a lizard, in which shape he could at least survive without water. 2. A warrior king of Argos (Argolis), grandson of Danaus and grandfather of Danaë, whose shield, originally belonging to his grandfather, had the power of reducing rebels to submission by the sight of it.

ABDERA A prosperous trading-port in Thrace, the inhabitants of which were a by-word for stupidity although they included the philosophers Protagoras and Democritus (*fl.* 5th cent. B.C.).

ABORIGINES In Roman tradition, not Stone Age man (of whom the Romans were unaware) and, significantly, *not* the Sicels (Siculi), the migrants from north Africa who moved via Sicily to southern Italy and the site of Rome, and ought literally to have been considered the aboriginals of Latium. The Romans used the term for the Villanovan tribes who drove the Siccls back to Sicily at about 1000 B.C. and became the progenitors of the Latini.

ABSYRTUS see APSYRTUS.

ABYDOS 1. A colonial town of Miletus on the south of the Hellespont at its narrowest part, north-east of Troy. The love-sick swimmer Leander lived there. 2. A city of upper Egypt where the so-called Table of Abydos was found, an inscription detailing the kings of Egypt, prior to Seti I (1318–1298 B.C.).

ABYLA (ABILA) The mountain on the south side of the strait of Gibraltar, opposite Calpe. The two rocks are the Pillars of Hercules.

ACADEMY (ACADEMIA) 1. A park on the river Cephisus on the west side of Athens, named after the hero Academus, where a gymnastic school was first established. 2. The college set up from his home near there by Plato, whose pupils became known as the Academic philosophers. The Academic college continued from 385 B.C. to A.D. 529.

ACARNANIA A state in north-west Greece colonised by Acarnan from Argos. Its inhabitants had a reputation for barbarous piracy and for skill with the sling.

ACASTUS The Argonaut son of Pelias, the usurping king of Iolcus and uncle of Jason who was cut up and boiled by his daughters on the suggestion by Medea that this operation would rejuvenate the old man. Acastus expelled from Iolcus both Medea and Jason, who had a title to the throne. As king, Acastus purified Peleus, his companion in the hunt for the Calydonian boar, for involuntary parricide during the confusion of that epic struggle. But the wife of Acastus, who had been sexually repulsed by Peleus, told Acastus that Peleus had tried to seduce her. Acastus challenged Peleus to a hunting contest and stole his magic sword, putting him in peril of his life on Mount Pelion. But Peleus came fortunately through his difficulties by marrying Thetis and siring Achilles, and eventually he killed Acastus and his wife.

ACCA LARENTIA Originally a Roman goddess, variously said to

have been a rich prostitute who left her property to the Romans or the successor to the she-wolf as the nurse of Romulus and Remus.

ACESTES The son of the river-god Crimisus and the noble Trojan refugee Egesta who founded Segesta in Sicily and welcomed Aeneas there.

ACHAEA Originally the area of Greece on the north of the Peloponnesus bordering the gulf of Corinth. Under Roman rule, after 146 B.C., it was the name of the province embracing all southern Greece as far as Thessaly. The ACHAEANS (Achaei) were an ancient Hellenic race originating from the north and modelling, with their nordic features, the so-called 'Greek god' type of manly beauty contrasting with the shorter and swarthier east-Mediterranean type. Homer referred to the Greeks collectively as Achaeans. The 4th-century ACHAEAN LEAGUE of 12 cities allied for mutual protection became politically important after 251 B.C. when membership was extended to include further cities including Corinth and eventually Sparta. As a negotiating power the league achieved considerable status *vis-à-vis* Macedonia, but fell to the Romans in 146 B.C.

ACHAEMENES Grandfather of Cyrus I and founder of the Persian imperial house which lasted from *c.* 600 B.C. until the death of Darius III in 330 B.C.

ACHARNAE The largest administrative area in Attica, north of Athens, with a lively population whose clashing interests in prosperity and belligerence were used by Aristophanes as the theme of his play *The Acharnians*.

ACHATES The faithful comrade of Aeneas.

ACHELOUS The longest river in Greece, running south from the Pindus mountains to the juncture of the gulf of Corinth with the Ionian sea; named after the god who was the father of all fresh waters.

ACHERON 1. A river in Epirus which occasionally runs underground. 2. A river of the lower world, its banks peopled by the shades.

ACHILLES A traditional hero of the Greeks and the literary hero of the *Iliad*. He was born and bred in Thessaly as the only mortal son of Peleus and the Nereid Thetis, at whose passionate wedding on Mount Pelion the principal gods of Olympia were present. Thetis consumed her first six sons in fire to make them immortal like herself, and would have done the same for Achilles, but Peleus snatched him from the ashes in time to preserve him, alive and invulnerable except for his right ankle which had not been immortalised. Thetis, in a rage, went back to live in the sea, but she did not altogether abandon Achilles, and revealed herself in influential visitations to him. Peleus entrusted the education of Achilles – he was to shine at hunting, fighting and fleetness of foot – to Chiron, the king of the centaurs and to Phoenix, a king's son who had been cursed with impotence. Achilles was also devoted to his older cousin Patroclus, but he had female as well as male lovers. He developed as an outstandingly martial prince to his father, who was king of the Myrmidons in Phthiotis. Although, at the instance of Thetis, Achilles had been disguised as a girl to discourage his being recruited for the expedition to Troy, he went of his own free will to the Trojan war – a war in which the gods themselves were divided – knowing from a prophecy of his divine mother that by doing so he condemned himself to die young, if gloriously. It is a part of the high quality of the *Iliad* that Achilles lived with this constant knowledge and also that, although a fighting hero, he had damaging faults of oversensitivity and exaggerated anger as well as the gentler, unheroic virtues of domesticity and a strong attraction to his mother. Amid many exploits during the ten-year siege of Troy, including the killing of Troilus, after whom he lusted, Achilles distinguished himself militarily until his commander-in-chief Agamemnon slighted him by requisitioning his concubine Briseis, after which Achilles sulked in his tent and the fortunes of the Achaeans declined. But Patroclus finally took over his forces and was killed in battle. Achilles, after a passion of grief, resumed the fighting, killed Hector, and ceremonially dragged his body around the tomb of Patroclus before restoring it to Priam of Troy. But Apollo, particularly incensed among many other actions by the killing of Troilus, directed the arrow of Paris which shot Achilles in his vulnerable right heel. The hero died in agony, and Thetis transported him to an island where he was believed to live in marriage with Helen.

ACIS A Sicilian shepherd, the son of Faunus, who loved the sea-nymph

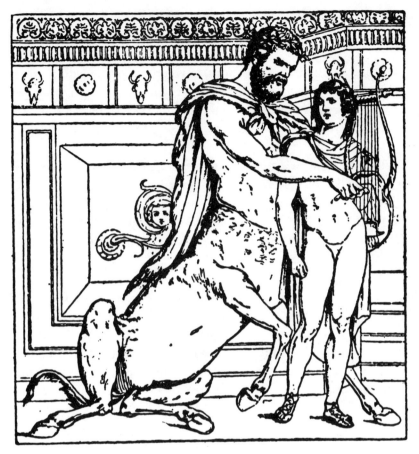

ACHILLES AND CHIRON.

Galatea and was crushed by a rock hurled by the Cyclops Polyphemus, who also desired her. He was transformed into the Sicilian river Acis.

ACONTIUS A youth of Ceos who, to win the maiden Cydippe, threw to her on Delos an apple on which was written 'I swear by the sanctuary of Diana to marry Acontius.' Cydippe read the message aloud, and Diana compelled her to keep the vow.

ACRISIUS King of Argos and father of Danaë, who cast away his daughter and her son Perseus, conceived by Zeus.

ACROCERAUNIA A promontory, dangerous to mariners, ending in Cape Glossa in northern Epirus. Shelley placed the snowy couch of Arethusa there.

ACROPOLIS A central fortified rock for the security of a Greek city. The Acropolis of Athens originally contained the palace of the first kings and a temple of Athena. After destruction by the Persians the Acropolis was rebuilt in the 5th century B.C. with the Parthenon (then containing an enormous statue of Athena), the temple of Athena Nike, the Erectheum (a shrine to a fabled king of Athens) and the Propylaea (the Porch).

ACROSTIC A set of verses or lines in which the initial letters spell intelligible sense, used by Plautus in the arguments preceding his comedies, by early Christian and later classical writers, and in an abecedarian form in Hebrew poems including Psalm CXIX.

ACTAEON The son of Aristaeus and Autonoë, a daughter of Cadmus, a skilful hunter after being trained by Chiron king of the Centaurs, who surprised Artemis bathing with her nymphs and was transformed into a stag for the impiety, and was torn to pieces by his fifty hounds on Mount Cithaeron.

ACTIUM A town and promontory in Acarnania in the Ambracian gulf of the Ionian sea off which Augustus won the naval battle against Antony and Cleopatra on 2 September 31 B.C. The town is now called Akri. The promontory held a temple to Apollo.

ADMETUS A king of Pherae in Thessaly to whom Pelias promised the hand of his daughter Alcestis if Admetus came to claim her in a chariot drawn by a lion and a boar, a feat which Admetus was enabled to perform because his beauty and piety had endeared him to Apollo, who was undergoing banishment on Earth at the time. At the bridal feast Admetus forgot to sacrifice to Artemis (as Oeneus did, and endured the ravages of the Calydonian boar), and realised that he was doomed. Apollo approached the Fates (Moirai), made them drunk and got them to promise that Admetus could live if anyone would voluntarily die in his stead. Alcestis made this sacrifice, but Heracles harrowed Hell and brought her back.

ADONIS A handsome youth, the son of Theias king of Syria and of Myrrha the daughter of Theias, with whom Aphrodite became infatuated. Adonis was killed while hunting, either by the jealous Hephaestus or by a boar, who may have been Ares in animal shape. From his blood sprang the anémone flower. Aphrodite mourned Adonis so keenly that the gods called a dispensation on death and allowed the youth to spend part of each year with Aphrodite. His death and resurrection were celebrated in the cult of the winter-spring rhythm of nature.

ADRASTUS The son of Talaus, king of Argos, who became king of Sicyon, returned to Argos and engineered two successive wars of 'The Seven Against Thebes'.

ADRIA 1. A Greek colony near the mouth of the Po from which the Adriatic sea took its name. 2. A Roman colony on the Adriatic where the family of the emperor Hadrian lived.

ADULE (ADULIS) An Ethiopian town on the Red Sea where was found the *Monumentum Adulitanum*, a Greek inscription of the conquests of Ptolemy III Euregetes.

AEACUS Son of Zeus and Aegina and king of the Myrmidons, so renowned for justice that he became one of the three judges of the dead in Hades.

AEDILES Roman magistrates supervising public buildings, street and market sanitation, public games and the policing of weights and measures and money-exchange.

AEDON The wife of Zethus, king of Thebes, who in envy of her sister-in-law Niobe's family of twelve resolved to kill Niobe's eldest son. In error she murdered her own son Itylus and her constant lamentation induced Zeus to change her into a nightingale.

AEDUI A powerful tribe in Gaul who were accepted by the Romans as blood-brothers.

AEËTES The king of Colchis who was father to Medea and Apsyrtus.

AEGEAN SEA That part of the Mediterranean between Greece and Asia Minor, subdivided into the Thracian sea in the north, the Myrtoan in the west, the Icarian in the east, and the Cretan in the south.

AEGEUS The son of Pandion and father of Theseus, who restored him to the kingship of Athens. When Theseus went to Crete to deliver Athens from the tribute to the Minotaur he promised to hoist white sails on his return, but forgot, and Aegeus, seeing black sails, threw himself into the sea which, according to some accounts, is named after him.

AEGINA An island in the Saronic gulf south-east of Athens, commercially very active, striking the silver tortoises which became the first Greek coinage, and also maintaining a long artistic tradition. Conquered and colonised by Athens in the 5th century B.C.

AEGIS Originally the thundercloud used by Zeus, later the goatskin cape manipulated by Athena to manifest power.

AEGISTHUS The son of Thyestes by his daughter Pelopia who killed Atreus and restored Thyestes to the throne of Mycenae. During the Trojan war he seduced Clytemnestra, wife of Agamemnon, and later killed Agamemnon but was killed by Orestes, son of Agamemnon.

AEGYPTUS King of Egypt, had fifty sons who followed the fifty daughters of his twin brother Danaus to Argos and demanded them in marriage. Danaus instructed his daughters to stab their husbands to death on the bridal night, and all were killed except Lynceus, who was saved by Hypermnestra.

AELIA (COLONIA AELIA CAPITOLINA) The name given to the new Jerusalem, rebuilt by the emperor Hadrian (Aelius Hadrianus) in A.D. 135 after having been razed by Titus in A.D. 70. No Jew was allowed to enter it.

AELIAN (CLAUDIUS AELIANUS) A popular philosopher (A.D. 170–235) from Praeneste, noted for his purity of diction.

AEMILIA (VIA AEMILIA) The road built by Marcus Aemilius Lepidus, consul 187 B.C., continuing the Via Flaminia from Ariminum (modern Rimini) to Mediolanum (Milan) in the pacification of Cisalpine Gaul. A later spur went to Aquileia (modern Venice).

AENEAS The Trojan war-lord in Homer's *Iliad* and, in Virgil's *Aeneid* the Trojan hero who settled in Latium and so gave the Romans their required ancestry from a historic people who were enemies of Greece. Aeneas was the son of Aphrodite and of Anchises, of the junior branch of the royal house of Troy. He came late into the Trojan war and at first sulked against Priam while others were fighting. Later, although valiant, he needed the luck he gained in attracting the gods to rescue him in extremities, particularly from certain death at the hands of Achilles. As Achilles knew he was eventually doomed by the gods, Aeneas had the counter-assurance that he was protected and would found a royal house. He took his ailing father and the images of his gods from Troy to Mount Ida, thence to Epirus, Sicily and north Africa, where he inspired the love of Dido of Carthage. He sailed to Latium, married Lavinia, the daughter of Latinus king of the Aborigines, and killed Turnus, who was betrothed to Lavinia. He died in a later battle and ascended into heaven, becoming a paternal god of the Latins.

AEOLIAN ISLANDS Seven islands based on Lipara (now Lipari) north-east of Sicily, secondarily named after Aeolus, demi-god of the winds, colonised from Cnidos and Rhodes, notorious as a haunt of pirates before becoming a Carthaginian base, finally captured by Rome in

HYGEA, AESCULAPIUS, AND TELESPHORUS.

252 B.C. Hephaestus was said to have his workshop on Hiera (now Vulcano). Strongyle (now Stromboli) was then less active.

AEOLUS 1. Mortal son of Poseidon who could parcel the winds in his floating island of Aeolia. 2. Son of Hellen, ancestor of the Aeolian branch of the Greeks, father of many children including Sisyphus.

AEQUI An ancient people in the central Apennines, subdued by the Romans in 431 and exterminated in 304 B.C.

AEROPE The mother of Agamemnon and Menelaus, either by her husband Plisthenes or his father Atreus.

AESCHINES An Athenian orator and statesman, 389–*c.* 332 B.C., political opponent of Demosthenes.

AESCHYLUS Tragic poet writing from Athens and Syracuse, born at Eleusis in Attica 525 B.C., died at Gela, Sicily in 456 B.C. by an oracular 'blow from heaven', a stork dropping a tortoise to break on his bald head, mistaking it for a stone. He fought at Marathon, Salamis and Plataea between writing his mature tragedies, and gained the prize for his trilogy *The Persae*, later being defeated in the contest by Sophocles. He introduced dialogue (as against declamation), opulent staging and impressive costume and dancing into Greek drama. His themes concern the will of man worked on by the decisions of the gods.

AESCULAPIUS (the commoner, latinised, form of **ASCLEPIUS**) Originally a heroic physician, later seen as the god of medicine, son of Apollo and pupil of Chiron. He extended his healing art to the resurrection of the dead, and after the resuscitation of Hippolytus Zeus jealously killed him with a thunderbolt. The religious cult of Aesculapius mixed medicine with magic. Based on Epidaurus, it was brought to Rome in 293 B.C. The god is usually portrayed with a staff, a serpent often coiled around it, attended by a dog and sometimes his children Hygieia and Panacea. The cock pledged to Asclepius by the dying Socrates was a traditional sacrifice.

AESOP (AESOPUS) Composer of fables moralising from stories about animals, *fl.* 570 B.C., born in Phrygia in north-west Asia Minor, freed from slavery in Samos, sent by Croesus, king of Lydia as an envoy to Delphi, where he was thrown from a precipice. His works were popular in Athens but no authentic originals survive.

AESOPUS CLAUDIUS *fl.* 1st half of 1st century B.C., was the greatest tragic actor of Rome, an elder contemporary of Roscius, and taught elocution to Cicero.

AETHIOPIA A powerful monarchy south of Egypt, at times dominating Egyptian civilisation, militarily defeated but never conquered by the Romans, adopted Christianity at a very early stage, possibly through the influence of the queen's eunuch mentioned in *Acts* VIII.

A ËTION Artist famous for his painting of the wedding of Alexander the Great and Roxana (327 B.C.).

AETNA The volcano in Sicily where two historic eruptions occurred in the 5th century B.C.

AETOLIA An area in Greece west and south of the river Achelous with outlets on the gulf of Corinth. The AETOLIAN LEAGUE was a considerable power in the 3rd century B.C.

AFRANIUS A Roman playwright of comic realism. *fl. c.* 100 B.C.

AFRICA A name not used by the Greeks, originally applied by the Romans to their province in modern north Africa, afterwards extended to the entire continent of what had previously been known as Libya – a reversal of modern terminology.

AFRICUS The south-west wind.

AGAMEDES Architect with his brother Trophonius of a treasury built for Hyreius, a king in Boeotia, from which they could remove riches at will through a secret aperture. The brothers also built the temple of Apollo at Delphi.

AGAMEMNON Son or grandson of Atreus, king of Mycenae, who after the murder of Atreus went to Sparta and married Clytemnestra, returned to be king of Mycenae, and became the strongest prince in Greece. After Paris abducted Helen, the wife of his brother Menelaus and sister of Clytemnestra, he led the Greek forces which were to invest Troy. He incurred the wrath of Artemis and agreed to sacrifice his daughter Iphigenia to her, but Artemis preserved the girl. His quarrel with Achilles provides the main plot of the *Iliad*. After the capture of Troy he took Cassandra as his prize. Returning home, he was murdered by Aegisthus, who had seduced Clytemnestra, and was avenged by his son Orestes.

AGATHOCLES 360–289 B.C., tyrant of Syracuse from 317 and later ruler of all that part of Sicily not submitting to Carthage. He invaded Africa and proclaimed himself king of Sicily, the only Hellenistic king among western Greeks.

AGATHON Notably handsome Athenian poet who won his first prize for tragic drama in 416 B.C. and in celebration gave a feast which was described by his friend Plato in the Symposium.

AGESILAUS 444–360 B.C., king of Sparta from 398, waged almost constant warfare in Asia Minor, the Grecian mainland and Egypt.

AGIS Name of the son of the founding prince of Sparta and of three kings who ruled Sparta in the 5th, 4th and 3rd centuries B.C.

AGONES The 'games' held in Greek cities, notably at Athens (the Dionysia and the Panathenaea), Corinth (the Isthmian games), Delphi (the Pythian games), Nemea and Olympia: principally athletic contests, but at Athens primarily contests in dramatic composition.

AGORA The market place in a Greek city where assemblies were held.

AGORACRITUS A pupil of Phidias and probably the sculptor of the colossal head of Nemesis (perhaps designed as Aphrodite) in the British Museum.

AGRAULOS Grand-daughter of Actaeus, first king of Athens, who threw herself from the Acropolis because an oracle demanded a self-sacrifice for Athens.

AGRICOLA (GNAEUS JULIUS AGRICOLA) From his early twenties (i.e., from A.D. 60) served in the military government of Britain, Asia and Aquitania in addition to posts in Rome culminating in the consulship, 77, and seven years as governor of Britain, 78–85. His biography by his son-in-law Tacitus is extant.

AGRIGENTUM (ACRAGAS to the Greeks) Imposing town in south Sicily colonised by Dorians from Gela c. 580 B.C., destroyed by Carthage 405, rebuilt and still displaying relics of its glory. Empedocles was born here.

AGRIPPA I (HERODES AGRIPPA) 'Agrippa the Great', grandson of Herod the Great, lived 10 B.C. – A.D. 44, was educated in Rome and became the friend of Caligula and Claudius. Caligula made him king of four tetrarchies in the east and Claudius advanced him to be king of Judaea and Samaria. He ordered the execution of the apostle James and the imprisonment of Peter.

AGRIPPA II Son of Herod Agrippa, was king of Chalcis from A.D. 50 and was later given extended authority. The apostle Paul pleaded his legal defence before him in 60. He took the Roman side in the war against the Jews ending 70, and retired to Rome, dying in A.D. 100.

AGRIPPA (MARCUS VIPSANIUS AGRIPPA) Was 19 years old when Julius Caesar was murdered in 44 B.C. and he supported Octavius (later Augustus), commanding the fleet at Actium in 31 and finally marrying Augustus' daughter Julia in 21. Three times consul, he built the Pantheon at his own expense. He died in 12 B.C.

AGRIPPINA (VIPSANIA AGRIPPINA), c. 40 B.C. – A.D. 20, daughter of Agrippa by his first marriage, married to Tiberius, stepson of Augustus, who in 12 B.C. was forced by Augustus to divorce her and marry Augustus' daughter Julia, (that is, Agrippina's step mother), newly widowed by the death of Agrippa.

AGRIPPINA MAJOR (VIPSANIA AGRIPPINA), *c.* 14 B.C. –
A.D. 33, daughter of Agrippa and Julia and grand-daughter of Augustus,
married to Germanicus A.D. 5, lived happily and heroically with her
soldier husband for 14 years until his death and bore him nine children,
including Gaius (Caligula) and Agrippina Minor. She spent the years
A.D. 19–30 in widowhood in Rome, becoming too respected and possibly
influential to please the emperor Tiberius who had been married both to
her stepsister and her mother and whom she suspected, with his mother
Livia, of having brought about her husband's death. She was exiled in 30
and starved herself to death in 33.

AGRIPPINA MINOR (JULIA AGRIPPINA), A.D. 15–59,
daughter of Agrippina Major, sister of Caligula and mother of Nero,
ultimate wife of Claudius, who she poisoned in 54 in order that Nero
should supplant Claudius' son Britannicus. Nero had his mother murdered
five years later.

AHENOBARBUS The name of an ancient Roman family, particu-
larly distinguished as soldiers and statesmen in the 150 years after 122 B.C.
Four were named Gnaeus Domitius Enobarbus, of whom the last married
Julia Agrippina in A.D. 32 and was the father of Nero. Ahenobarbus signi-
fied Redbeard.

AIDES (AIDONEUS) see HADES.

AIUS LOCUTIUS An unknown voice which warned that the Gauls
were advancing on Rome in 390 B.C., to which a shrine was later dedicated.

AJAX (the commoner, latinised, form of AIAS) 1. The son of Telamon
king of Salamis, a reliable bulwark of a warrior distinguished by a huge
shield, who took 12 ships to Troy and was surpassed in courage only by
Achilles, whose armour he lost to Odysseus after the death of Achilles, a
disappointment which drove him mad. 2. The son of Oileus king of the
Locrians who took 40 ships to Troy, a soldier second only to Achilles in
swiftness of foot, portrayed as a charmless, god-defying man who ravished
Cassandra in the temple of Athena after the fall of Troy but was later cast
by Poseidon into the sea to drown.

ALABANDA A caravan-crossroad city in Asia Minor noted for its wealth and depravity.

ALANI An Asiatic Scythian people who menaced Europe for the first three centuries A.D. and were finally swept westwards by the Huns following from behind and passed into Gaul and Spain.

ALARICUS The king of the Visigoths who captured Rome in A.D. 410 and shortly afterwards died.

ALBA LONGA The most ancient town in Latium built on the Alban Hills 12 miles from Rome, destroyed *c.* 600 B.C. and never rebuilt, though the area was appropriated for the villas of the aristocracy.

ALBION Ancient name for Britain (excluding Ireland) superseded by the name Britannia.

ALCAEUS Soldier and lyric poet of Mytilene in Lesbos from whose name the Alcaic metre derives, *fl.* 600 B.C.

ALCESTIS The wife of ADMETUS, whom see.

ALCIBIADES Athenian general and statesman, *c.* 450–404 B.C., the ward of Pericles and intimate of Socrates, who saved his life in battle and who later was similarly rescued by Alcibiades. A handsome and dissolute maverick general who was murdered by conspirators in Phrygia.

ALCMAN A Lydian of Sardis, *fl.* 630 B.C., who became the principal lyric poet of Sparta and was said to have introduced the poetry of love.

ALCMENE Wife of Amphitryon the son of Alcaeus, who refused her husband conjugal privileges until he had avenged the death of her brothers. In his absence on this mission Zeus visited Alcmene in the shape of Amphitryon, recounted details of a revenge taken, and sired Heracles on her. She bore Iphicles to Amphitryon.

ALCYONE (HALCYONE) Daughter of Aeolus, became the wife of Ceyx who died in a shipwreck. She cast herself in grief into the sea but the couple were changed into birds, and at the breeding time of the halcyon the sea is always calm.

ALEMANNI A confederation of tribes in Germany active from the 3rd to the 5th centuries A.D.

ALEXANDER 1. The name of three kings of Macedonia. Alexander I reigned c. 505–455 B.C. Alexander II reigned 369–367 B.C. Alexander III, Alexander the Great, son of Philip II, was born at Pella in 356 B.C. and was educated by Aristotle. He succeeded in 336, marched into Greece and prepared to lead the Greek armies against the Persians after destroying the rebellious city of Thebes. He crossed the Hellespont in 334, cut the Gordian knot at Gordium in Phrygia, which oracularly marked him as the conqueror of Asia. He defeated Darius in 333, occupied Egypt in 332, founding Alexandria in 331, and marched again against Darius, crossing the Euphrates and the Tigris and defeating the Persians in the great battle of Gaugamela in Mesopotamia in October 331. He took Babylon, destroyed Persepolis, and learned of the murder of Darius in Parthia. Having crossed the Hindu Kush and married Roxana, daughter of the Bactrian chief Oxyartes, he invaded India and reached the Indian Ocean in 326. He died of a fever contracted through drink in Babylon in 323. 2. The name of two successive kings of Epirus who reigned from 336–272 B.C. 3. The name of two kings of Syria who reigned in the second century B.C.

ALEXANDRIA 1. Alexander's foundation of 331 B.C., designed as a naval base, which became the capital of Egypt under the Ptolemies, who built the famous lighthouse and the unique library, partially burnt by Julius Caesar and finally destroyed by the Moslems in A.D. 651. Alexandria became the greatest city in the Roman empire and the centre of Christian theology. 2. Alexandria Troas, south-west of Troy, considered by both Julius Caesar and Constantine as a potential capital of the empire. 3. Alexandria ad Issum (Alexandria of Cicilia), the port later called Alexandretta, now Iskanderun. 4. The name of four distinct cities founded by Alexander in Afghanistan, in the vicinity of the modern Kandahar, Herat and Kabul.

ALEXIS Comic playwright born at Thurii, southern Italy about 372 B.C. but for most of his long life living in Athens where he wrote possibly 245 plays. He introduced his nephew Menander to comedy-writing and died 270 B.C.

ALOEUS Son of Poseidon and husband of Iphimedeia who, however, was also coupled by Poseidon and produced her two sons Otus and Ephialtes, charitably called the Aloidae, who quickly grew to giant size and mischievous temperament and, after imprisoning Ares for thirteen months, decided to climb to heaven by piling Pelion on Ossa. Apollo contrived that they should kill each other, before their beards had grown, by shooting at a deer he sent between their paths.

ALPHEUS The principal river of the Peloponnesus, flowing through Arcadia and past Olympia and passing with fresh waters untainted by the sea from the Ionian sea to Arethusa's fountain at Ortygia, Syracuse, as the river-god Alpheus still pursued the nymph Arethusa.

ALTIS The sacred grove where the Olympic games were held.

ALYATTES Conquering king of Lydia, 615–560 B.C., father of Croesus. The huge circular barrow of his tomb can still be seen near Sardis.

AMALTHEA The nymph who nursed the suckling Zeus in Crete, when Zeus broke off the horn of a goat to produce the cornucopia.

AMAZONS (AMAZONES, AMAZONIDES) The mythical race of woman warriors, said to live in Asia Minor, and to cut off the right breast of their daughters so that they could be easier at archery.

AMBRACIA The Greek city north of the bay of Actium which was made the capital of Epirus by Pyrrhus.

AMBROSIA The food of the gods, but sometimes referred to as their drink, which was normally given as nectar.

AMMIANUS MARCELLINUS Accurate Roman historian, born c. A.D. 330, of whose work 18 books covering A.D. 353–378 are extant.

A FIGHTING AMAZON.

AMPHION AND ZETHUS.

AMMON The principal god of the Egyptians, whose worship originated in Thebes, Egypt.

AMPHION Twin brother with Zethus from Zeus and Antiope, exposed at birth and reared by a shepherd on Mount Cithaeron. In maturity they marched against Thebes and killed Lycus, the mortal husband of Antiope, who had treated her cruelly. They built a wall round Thebes, Amphion drawing the stones into position by the music of a lyre given him by Hermes. Amphion married Niobe, and when their many children were jealously murdered he destroyed himself.

AMYCUS King of the savage Bebryces in Bithynia, a son of Poseidon who was an expert boxer, challenging and killing all strangers until the visiting Argonauts put up their champion Polydeuces, who killed him.

ANACREON Sixth-century B.C. lyric poet of love and wine who died at 85 through choking on a grape-pip.

ANAXAGORAS Controversial sage who migrated from Ionia to become the first philosopher to reside in Athens, 480 B.C. An associate of Euripides, he was put on trial for impiety in 450 and saved from the death sentence by the eloquence of his friend Pericles. He went into exile and died in 428. His impiety consisted in proclaiming the supremacy of intelligence.

ANCAEUS The name of two Argonauts: 1. the son of Lycurgus of Arcadia, killed by the Calydonian boar; 2. the son of Poseidon who took the helm of the Argo after the death of Tiphys.

ANCHISES Grandson of Ilus and cousin of Priam, king of Dardanus on Mount Ida where his beauty captivated Aphrodite and he sired on her Aeneas. But he disobeyed the command of the goddess to keep silent about the affair and he was blinded, or some say lamed, by her. After the fall of Troy Aeneas carried Anchises on his shoulders to his ship and brought him to Sicily, where he died.

ANCYRA Later Angora, now Ankara. Had a temple dedicated by the Galatians to Rome and Augustus which contained the *Monumentum*

Ancyranum (still extant), a marble inscription of the exploits of Augustus, duplicating the bronze tablets ordered by the emperor to be cut in Rome.

ANDROCLUS (ANDROCLES) A runaway slave brought to Rome from Africa and condemned to be delivered to the beasts in the circus. A lion in the arena held out his paw to him, recognising Androcles as the man who had extracted a thorn from it in Africa, after which they had lived together. Androcles was reprieved and given the lion, which he would take round Rome on a lead.

ANDROGEUS (ANDROGEOS) A son of Minos and Pasiphae who was slaughtered by Aegeus in Athens after winning the Panathenaea. Minos thereupon subdued Athens and exacted the annual tribute of seven youths and seven damsels for sacrifice to the Minotaur.

ANDROMACHE The wife of Hector whose son Astyanax was hurled from the walls of Troy during the sacking. She became the prize of Neoptolemus, son of Achilles, but afterwards married Helenus, Hector's brother.

ANDROMEDA The daughter of Cepheus king of Ethiopia and of Cassiope, chained by her father to a rock as a sacrifice to a ravaging sea-monster sent by Poseidon, rescued by Perseus who married her after killing her uncle Phineus, previously betrothed to her.

ANTICLEA The mother of Odysseus, either by her husband Laertes or by Sisyphus with whom she had previously lived. She died of grief before her son returned.

ANTIGONE The daughter of Oedipus by his mother Jocasta. She remained with her blinded father until his death and later defied Creon, who walled her in a cave, where she killed herself.

ANTINOUS 1. A suitor of Penelope, killed by Odysseus. 2. Favourite of the emperor Hadrian, drowned in the Nile A.D. 122, after which Hadrian made him a god.

ANTIOCH (ANTIOCHIA) The name of several cities east of the

Mediterranean, notably the capital of the Greek kingdom of Seleucid Syria, later the see of a Christian patriarch.

ANTIOCHUS The name of a great number of Seleucid kings of Syria, 280–65 B.C.

ANTIPATER 1. A Macedonian general, appointed by Alexander regent of Macedonia in 334 B.C. 2. Father of Herod the Great, procurator of Judaea 47–43 B.C. 3. Heir of Herod the Great, executed for conspiracy five days before Herod's death in 4 B.C. (the year of the birth of Jesus).

ANTIPHON The first Attic orator, 480–411 B.C., who composed speeches for others, delivering only one himself, which failed to save him from condemnation to death.

ANTISTHENES A follower of Socrates and founder of the Cynic philosophers, *fl*. 400 B.C.

ANTIUM A summer resort for Romans, the birthplace of Nero, modern Anzio.

ANTONINUS PIUS (TITUS AURELIUS FULVUS BOIONIUS ANTONINUS) A.D. 86–161, adopted by Hadrian and succeeded him as emperor in 138, a wholly beneficent ruler.

ANTONIUS (MARCUS ANTONIUS) Mark Antony, the triumvir, 82–30 B.C., developed as a cavalry commander after a wild youth and joined Julius Caesar's staff in Gaul, later supporting him in the Senate. Consul with Julius at the time of Caesar's death in 44, he intrigued for what power he could father from the assassination but finally joined Octavian (Augustus) and Lepidus in a five-year triumvirate. He defeated Brutus and Cassius at Philippi in 42 and was awarded suzerainty over Asia. He met Cleopatra at Tarsus in 41 and followed her to Egypt. His wife Fulvia and his brother Lucius made unsuccessful war against Octavian, but Fulvia died and Antony married Octavia, sister to Octavian. After the defeat of Pompey and the renewal of the triumvirate Antony returned to his eastern territories but in 37 sent Octavia to Rome and devoted himself to Cleopatra. Gradually assuming the role of an independent eastern despot, Antony was finally challenged by Octavian and defeated at Actium in 31. He retired with Cleopatra to Alexandria, where he committed suicide when Octavian pursued him there in 30. Cleopatra, his fifth wife if the marriage had been recognised, bore him three children, Alexander, Ptolemy and Cleopatra.

APELLES Painter from Colophon, Asia Minor who studied at Ephesus and then at Sicyon in the Peloponnesus, long the centre of Greek art. A contemporary and friend of Alexander the Great, who would sit for no other portrait painter. He painted a notable *Aphrodite Rising from the Sea* which Augustus took to Rome three centuries later.

APHRODITE Greek goddess of fertility, and thence of sexual love and of beauty, having many affinities with the Phoenician Astarte and the Babylonian Ishtar, primitive also in the death-in-life concept of her birth by rising from the foam created when the genitals of Uranus, the First Father, were cast into the sea after his castration by his son Cronus incited by Ge (Mother Earth): since Cronus was in turn dethroned by Zeus, his son, the myth makes Aphrodite more ancient and more essential than Zeus. Later sophistication of the story regularised it into recounting that Aphrodite was the daughter of Zeus and Dione and was married to Hephaestus, who she cuckolded by an intermittent infatuation with Ares and more casual affairs with the gods Hermes (by whom she bore Hermaphroditus), Dionysus (who sired Priapus, grossly distorted by the disapproving Hera) and Poseidon, and the mortals Anchises and Adonis. Her son Eros was not fathered by Hephaestus, but by one of the gods, possibly even Zeus. She was judged by Paris the most beautiful of the goddesses, though Zeus offered a choice only of Hera, Athena and herself and Aphrodite did, at Athena's request, remove the girdle which caused any beholder to fall in love with her; and she did bribe Paris by offering to procure Helen and thus beginning the Trojan war. Aphrodite, born in the foam, stepped ashore from a scallop shell at Cythera but later favoured Cyprus, where her worship at Paphos was most intense and where she would renew her virginity in the sea.

APIS The sacred bull at Memphis, a living god of the Egyptians.

APOLLO The Greek god whose worship was paramount in shaping the

APHRODITE, OR VENUS.

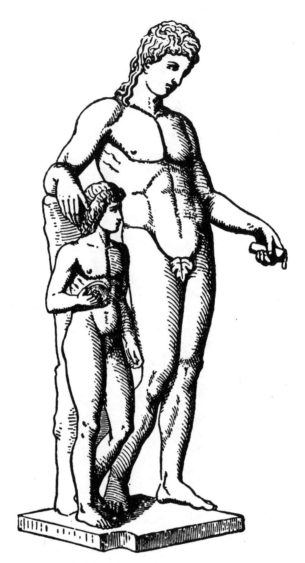

APOLLO AND HYACINTHUS.

character of Greek civilisation: the deity of beneficent power, of righteous punishment, of prophecy and music, of prosperous cattle-raising and the establishment of cultured communities in cities, and of manly beauty of the northern, Achaean, type. The son of Zeus and Leto, he was twin-born with Artemis. But Artemis was born on the island of Ortygia (later called Rhenaia, modern Megali Dili) and as soon as she was delivered she helped her mother to cross the narrow strait to Delos, and there Apollo was born. Delos was until then a floating island, but it was securely chained to the sea-bed by Zeus for the safe delivery of his son: to this day Delos is so sacred that no one may be born or die there, and the parturient and the sick are ferried to Megali Dili, and no one may stay there at night. Apollo was a lively child, who called for bow and arrows on the fourth day of his life and killed his mother's enemy, the serpent Python, at Delphi. He took over the Delphic oracle and its priestess, the Pythoness. He became accomplished at singing to the music of his lyre. He was moderately lecherous, though he never married, and he had one infatuation with the youth Hyacinth. When Zeus killed Asclepius, Apollo's son by Coronis, for robbing Hades of his dead by resuscitation, Apollo killed the Cyclopes in revenge. Zeus would have banished Apollo to Tartarus for ever, but he relented and sentenced him to a year's hard labour tending the flocks of Admetus. Apollo mildly served his time and never again revolted against Zeus, always counselling moderation in all things.

APOLLODORUS 1. Athenian painter, *fl.* 430 B.C., the first to abandon flat delineation and to show light and shade and the gradation of colour. 2. Athenian comic playwright working from 285 B.C.

APOLLONIUS The name of a number of writers, sculptors, rhetoricians and grammarians.

APPIA (VIA APPIA) The road initiated by Appius Claudius Caecus when censor in 312 B.C. leading south from Rome to Capua and eventually to Brundusium (modern Brindisi).

APSYRTUS The son of Acëtes king of Colchis. Medea was the daughter of Acëtes by another wife. When Medea fled with Jason she took Apsyrtus with her and, to delay her father in his pursuit, killed her half-brother and

[33]

dismembered him, casting pieces of the body on the road for Aeëtes to gather.

APULEIUS Widely travelled rhetorician and dabbler in magic whose speech defending himself from a charge of having used magic to marry a rich widow, delivered at Sabrata near Tripoli *c.* A.D. 157, is extant, as is his *Metamorphoses* (*The Golden Ass*), the delightful, unique Latin novel.

AQUAE SULIS A spa established in the 1st century A.D., modern Bath.

AQUILEIA A strategic and commercial stronghold at the head of the Adriatic, founded 181 B.C., destroyed by Attila A.D. 452, when its inhabitants fled to establish modern Venice. Because of its military character as a garrison town Aquileia was a centre of Mithraism.

AQUINUM Modern Aquino, near Naples, the birthplace of Juvenal and St. Thomas Aquinas.

AQUITANIA The territory from the Pyrenees to the Garumna (Garonne), later Aquitaine including Gascony.

ARABIA To the ancients, the country between the Red Sea, the Indian Ocean and the Persian Gulf. Arabia Petraea, the area north of the Red Sea based on Petra became a Roman province.

ARABICUS SINUS The Red Sea.

ARACHNE Daughter of Idmon of Colophon in Lydia, a skilled weaver and dyer who challenged Athena, weaving a tapestry portraying the amours of the gods which Athena spitefully destroyed. Arachne hanged herself but Athena changed her into a spider and the rope into a cobweb.

ARCADIA Mountainous country in the central Peloponnesus famous for the bucolic simplicity of its life.

ARCHELAUS 1. A 5th century B.C. philosopher. 2. King of Macedonia 413–399 B.C. 3. A. Greek general of Mithridates VI defeated by

ARES, OR MARS.

Sulla in Bocotia in 86 B.C. 4. Son of the last-named, briefly king of Egypt in 55 B.C. 5. Grandson of the last-named; his mother Glaphyra seduced Mark Antony into giving him the kingdom of Cappadocia in 36 B.C. but Tiberius unseated him in A.D. 17. 6. Son and heir of Herod the Great, succeeding him in 4 B.C., deposed and banished by Augustus in A.D. 7.

ARCHIDAMUS The name of five kings of Sparta, of whom Archidamus II invaded Attica three times from 431 B.C.

ARCHILOCHUS Lyric poet of Paros, *fl.* 700 B.C., whose lampoons were so deadly that a poem attacking a girl who had jilted him made her and all her sisters hang themselves in shame.

ARCHIMEDES Mathematician, philospher and military engineer living at Syracuse 287-212 B.C. whose inventions include the Screw of Archimedes for raising water.

ARCHON In general, an office-holder in a Greek city; in Athens, a member of the council of nine which took over the prerogatives of the former royal house.

AREOPAGUS The criminal court in Athens particularly concerned with homicide, grievous bodily harm and arson, which sat on the Areopagus, the hill of Ares, near the Acropolis.

ARES A strangely unsympathetic god in the Greek theogony, reflecting the Greek distaste for war when waged for its own sake without a cause. The son of Zeus and Hera, born a twin with Eris who became his matching goddess of Strife, Ares developed as a drunken and quarrelsome god of war, but was defeated in three notable fights – twice being almost mortally wounded (but he was immortal) by Heracles, and once being imprisoned for 13 months by the Aloidae before the assault on Olympus. Aphrodite had an inexplicable passion for him, and was trapped in bed with him by her husband Hephaestus, who had designed a metal net to fall on them from the bedposts and put the couple on show for the Olympians. He fathered three children on Aphrodite and scores in other encounters, but there is no attractive suggestion of affection in any of his recorded affairs. Astrologers assigned to him the planet of growth (see MARS) and calendarists made Tuesday his day.

ARETHUSA A Nereid desired by **ALPHEUS**, whom see; the nymph of the fountain of Arethusa in the island of Ortygia off Syracuse (not the island near Delos).

ARGONAUTS The fifty heroes who sailed in the *Argo*, the boat built by Argos, to snatch the golden fleece sought by **JASON**, whom see.

ARGOS (ARGOLIS) An area in the eastern Peloponnesus, once the kingdom ruled by Atreus and Agamemnon with their capital at Mycenae, but also containing the city of Argos which later overshadowed Mycenae and became second only to Sparta in political importance. Heraeum, the great temple of Hera, was built between Argos and Mycenae.

ARGUS 1. The hundred-eyed monster set by Hera to guard Io, whom Zeus had turned into a heifer to put Hera (unsuccessfully) off the scent of his lusting. Argus was killed by Hermes at Zeus' request, and Hera put his eyes into the spread of her favourite bird, the peacock. 2. The faithful dog of Odysseus who died with joy when his master came home.

ARIADNE The daughter of Minos and Pasiphaë who contrived the means for her lover Theseus to escape from the Labyrinth after killing the Minotaur and, eloping with him from Crete, was abandoned on Naxos, where Dionysus found her and quickly married her, giving her a bridal crown which he later set among the stars.

ARION 1. A lyric poet of Lesbos and virtuoso on the cithara (a more sonorous version of the lyre), *fl.* 625 B.C., who developed the dithyramb (a form of choral song) and had the reputation of having been brought back to his Corinth home by a dolphin when piratical sailors threw him in the sea for his treasures. 2. A talking horse, the offspring of Poseidon and Demeter whose speed saved Adrastus when the Seven fought Thebes.

ARISTAEUS Son of Apollo and Cyrene, pursued Eurydice, the wife of Orpheus, who in her flight received a snake-bite and died. In retribution the Nymphs destroyed the bees of Aristaeus. On the advice of Cyrene he sacrificed cattle to the Nymphs, and after nine days found bees swarming in their remains.

[37]

ARIADNE ABANDONED.

ARISTARCHUS A notable scholar from Samothace, 216–144 B.C., Keeper of the Library at Alexandria from 153, who published the seminal critical edition of Homer.

ARISTIDES 'The Just', Athenian soldier-statesman c.520–468 B.C.

ARISTOPHANES Athenian comic playwright, c.450–385 B.C., highly regarded and winning four dramatic contests, whose eleven extant plays show keen, almost moral, satire, alert situation comedy and knock-down farce soaring to pure lyric poetry in the choruses.

ARISTOTLE (ARISTOTELES) Philosopher and scientist, son of the physician to Amyntas II of Macedonia, born 384 B.C. at Stageira in Chalcidice (modern Stavro), entered Plato's Academy at Athens at the age of 17 and remained there until the death of Plato 20 years later, when with Xenocrates he moved to Mysia, later to Lesbos, thence to Macedon in 342 to take over the education of the 13-year-old Alexander. In 334 he founded the Lyceum in Athens in a grove dedicated to Apollo Lyceius (as god of light) where, striding and disputing with his Peripatetic Philosophers, he hammered out principles of logic and morals in the mornings, and lectured on rhetoric and politics in the evenings, still finding time to write the body of his works. Accused of impiety in 322 B.C., he evaded trial and died almost immediately in Chalcis in Euboea.

ARMINIUS (Latin form of HERMANN) 18 B.C. – A.D. 19, 'Liberator of the Germans' according to Tacitus, chief of the Cherusci tribe, which he enrolled as Roman auxiliaries until he rose against Roman occupation and by defeating Quinctilius Varus in A.D. 9 forced the Romans to retreat to the Rhine. Five years later Germanicus began an offensive but was jealously recalled by Tiberius when his success seemed certain. Arminius was conveniently assassinated by his own people.

ARSACIDS The royal dynasty of Parthia, 250 B.C. – A.D. 230, named after Arsaces I, who engineered the Parthian revolt against Antiochus king of Syria.

ARSINOË The name of a number of women in the royal house of

the Ptolemies of Egypt, including the sister of Cleopatra. It is also the name of a number of cities called after these ladies.

ARTAXERXES The name of four Persian kings between 464 B.C. and A.D. 241.

ARTAXIAS The name of three kings of Armenia between 190 B.C. and A.D. 35.

ARTEMIDORUS Ephesian-born citizen of Rome in the 2nd century A.D. who wrote an extant book on the interpretation of dreams, still valuable for its insight into the beliefs of the time.

ARTEMIS To the Greeks, not only the goddess who was the physical twin of Apollo, whom see, but also in many respects the spiritual twin, save that Artemis was a virgin unmoved by love and showed what could be considered a spinsterish spite, not only against such as Actaeon who had seen her bathing, but against the many mortals who at some time in the crises of their lives forgot to sacrifice to her.

ARTEMISIA I Princess of Caria, queen under Persian suzerainty of Halicarnassus, Cos, Nisyrus and Calyndus, exhibited enterprise, courage and prudence in the invasion of Greece by Xerxes and the battle of Salamis, 480 B.C.

ARTEMISIA II Princess of Caria and consort of Mausolus, at whose death in 350 B.C. she expressed the monumental grief exemplified in the Mausoleum of Halicarnassus, one of the seven wonders of the world.

ASCANIUS A son of Aeneas who founded Alba Longa. His significance is that the Romans called him Iulus, and the Julian clan – including Julius Caesar – claimed descent from Aeneas through him.

ASCLEPIUS See AESCULAPIUS.

ASIA Daughter of Oceanus and Tethys, and by Iapetus mother of Atlas, Prometheus and Epimetheus; also identified as Clymene.

ASIA (ASIS) To the Greeks, the farther part of Asia Minor, a connotation which was not adopted until the 4th century B.C. The Roman province of Asia comprised the coastal strip of Asia Minor.

ASPASIA The mistress of Pericles who, by wit rather than beauty, justified the geisha-courtesan institution of the Greek Hetaerae.

ASTYANAX The son of Hector and Andromache who was hurled from the walls of Troy to extinguish the royal line.

ATALANTA Daughter of Iasus of Arcadia and Clymene, exposed at birth because she was not a boy, suckled by a she-bear sent by Artemis, a goddess whom she was greatly to resemble in her aversion to marriage and her addiction to hunting, and with whom she was significantly connected by attending the hunt for the Calydonian boar, which Artemis had sent as a scourge because Oenus king of Calydon forgot one summer to sacrifice to her. At the boar hunt Atalanta shot dead two of the party who had decided to ravish her, and she scored first hit on the boar. This earned her recognition by her father, with the proviso that she must prepare to be married. An oracle had warned her that she must stay a virgin, and she stipulated that any suitor must first beat her in a foot race or be killed by her – and she killed many. But Aphrodite gave Melanion three golden apples which he was to drop at intervals during the race, and as Atalanta stooped to pick up the last lure Melanion beat her to the finish. She surrendered her virginity, but was persuaded by Melanion to copulate in a shrine of Cybele, for which impiety Cybele changed both into lions, which were then believed not to mate with lions but only with leopards, so that they could never savour each other again.

ATE Ancient Greek goddess of infatuation and the surrender of moral principles, the daughter of Eris the goddess of strife.

ATELLA A town 8 miles north of Naples, the home of the popular and coarse farces played in Rome called the Atellanae or Atellanae Fabulae. Later, under the name Aversa, it was the first place where the Normans settled in Italy, A.D. 1029.

ATHENA (ATHENE) A goddess adopted by the Athenians, probably from the Minoan-Mycenean religion, as the patron of the prince in his acropolis. This concept was developed for general acceptance by the Greeks into the more conformist notion of a goddess personifying wisdom who encourages industry, skill and intellectual pursuits, is benignly concerned with propagation although herself a virgin, and is the protective genius of the city-nation at war. The myth of the birth of Athena illustrates the compromises necessary in this progression of thought. Zeus desired intercourse with Metis, the Titaness of the first creation who governed the planet Mercury and the fourth day of the week and who was the source of all wisdom. He finally impregnated Metis, and the Earth Mother foretold that she would bear a daughter, but if she conceived again she would produce a son who would depose Zeus in the same way as Zeus had deposed his father Cronus and Cronus his father Uranus. Zeus therefore paid fresh court to Metis, and when she was conciliatory he suddenly swallowed her, though he still relied on her presence to give him counsels of wisdom. Later he was attacked by a fierce headache and his groans shook the world. Hermes persuaded Hephaestus to beat a wedge into the skull of Zeus, and Athena promptly sprang into the world, fully grown, fully armed and uttering a great war-cry. In this way matriarchy, the old source of wisdom, was conveniently reconciled with the sovereignty of Zeus.

ATHENAE Athens, the capital of ancient Attica, an area ruled by separate kings until about 900 B.C. In Athens and elsewhere the monarchical system was supplanted by an aristocracy, and a later immature struggle for democracy led first to tyranny before a democratic constitution was established in the 6th century B.C. The leading role taken by Athens in the wars against Persia consolidated her imperial supremacy in 5th century Greece, and in this period there came a great flowering of the arts and sciences. In the next century Athens was weakened by her resistance to Spartan imperialism but prosperity returned and the arts again flourished. However, in the third and second centuries the impact of Athens markedly diminished as the power of Rome gradually grew. In 146 B.C. Athens became part of the Roman empire and existed as a quiet university town.

ATHENAEUM A centre sacred to Athena, and in particular a school of literature and science established in Rome by Hadrian in A.D. 133.

PALLAS ATHENE, BY PHIDIAS.

ATHENAEUS Author, in about A.D. 200, of a miscellany of anecdotes and literary extracts, part of which is extant.

ATHOS (ACTE) Very high headland in Chalcidice, Macedonia, inducing dangerous storms, one of which destroyed a Persian fleet and inspired Xerxes to cut a canal across the mile-and-a-half isthmus, 483–481 B.C.

ATIA Niece of Julius Caesar and mother of Octavia and Octavius (later Augustus), the latter by Apollo according to Augustus' propaganda machine, by Caius Octavius according to the records.

ATLANTIS A beautiful island west of the Pillars of Hercules, inundated by the ocean when its inhabitants grew impious.

ATLAS Titan son of Iapetus and Clymene, father of the Pleiades, Hyades and Hesperides by Aethra daughter of Oceanus, after losing the Titan war against Zeus was sentenced to carry heaven on his head and hands.

ATOSSA Daughter of Cyrus, who died 529 B.C., wife of his successor, her brother Cambyses, then wife of Darius Hystaspis by whom she was the mother of Xerxes.

ATREUS Son of Pelops and Hippodameia, grandson of Tantalus and thus descended from Zeus, and an actor in a complicated web of tragedy. Atreus and his brother Thyestes had a half-brother Chrysippus who was abducted and introduced into pederasty by Laius king of Thebes. Hippodameia feared that Pelops preferred Chrysippus over her own sons and tried to persuade Atreus and Thyestes to kill him. They demurred, so Hippodameia herself stabbed Chrysippus with the sword of Laius while the two men were in bed. Atreus, in some guilt and confusion, fled with Thyestes to Mycenae, where he later became king but not before a dispute with Thyestes over the succession. Atreus had married as his second wife Aerope, who became the mother of Agamemnon and Menelaus, perhaps by Atreus but possibly by the son of Atreus' first marriage, Plisthenes. Aerope had an adulterous affair with Thyestes. Atreus consolidated his claim to the throne of Mycenae by making the sun retreat and set in the east – either by arrangement with Zeus or because Helios faltered in horror when Atreus served to Thyestes the flesh of his slaughtered children and then sent in their heads and extremities when Thyestes had eaten. (At a point in the story which varies with the teller Thyestes sent Plisthenes to murder Atreus, who foiled the attempt and killed Plisthenes.) Atreus killed Aerope. Thyestes cursed Atreus, sought refuge in Sicyon, and was told by the Delphic Oracle that it was necessary to beget a child on a daughter of his own, which he did by rape on Pelopia, a daughter who had become a priestess in Sicyon and did not recognise Thyestes in the dark. Atreus in his turn was told by the Delphic Oracle to recall Thyestes from banishment. Atreus sought Thyestes in Sicyon but he had fled. Atreus fell in love with Pelopia, whom he believed to be a princess of Sicyon, and asked to marry her. The king of Sicyon, who wanted Atreus as an ally, did not disclose her true parentage and agreed. Pelopia gave birth to Aegisthus and Atreus believed the boy to be his own child. Agamemnon and Menelaus later found Thyestes by chance and brought him to Mycenae. Atreus ordered Aegisthus, then seven years old, to kill Thyestes. Thyestes disarmed Aegisthus and, because of a particular sword that had been used, recognised Aegisthus as his own son. By the same token Pelopia understood that her ravisher had been her father, and killed herself. Aegisthus, at the command of Thyestes, killed Atreus.

ATROPOS The most decisive of the three Fates, the being who insists that the destiny her sisters have shaped must be carried out.

ATTICA The wedge-shaped area of Greece containing Athens, bounded on two sides by the Aegean, on the west by Megaris and on the north by Boeotia.

ATTICUS Titus Pomponius, 109–32 B.C., called Atticus because of long residence in Athens where he derived his great wealth from land-owning, banking and business. A friend of Cicero, a trimmer in politics and a devotee of culture.

ATTILA Born c. A.D. 400, succeeded as king of the Huns in 434, proclaimed himself in 445 king of the Barbarians between the German ocean and China, ravaged the eastern empire from that time and the western from 450, defeated by the Roman Aetius in alliance with Theodoric king

[45]

of the Visigoths (who was killed) in 451 at the battle of the Catalaunian Fields (thought to be near Chélons-sur-Marne and historically referred to as the battle of Chélons but probably fought near Troyes), regrouped and captured Aquileia in 452 but did not advance to Rome, died 453, probably poisoned.

AUGUSTA The name of a number of colonies founded by Augustus notably at Aosta, Turin, Trier and Augsburg.

AUGUSTINUS (AURELIUS AUGUSTINUS, Saint Augustine, in English, Austin) born Numidia, north Africa A.D. 354, spent many years at Carthage university, then Rome, then professor of rhetoric at Milan where he was baptised in 386. Returned to Numidia and took holy orders at Hippo there, becoming bishop in 395 and writing a great body of theological work until his death in 430.

AUGUSTULUS (ROMULUS AUGUSTULUS) The last Roman emperor of the west, deposed A.D. 476 by ODOACER, whom see.

AUGUSTUS (CAIUS OCTAVIUS, later when adopted by Caius Julius Caesar, brother of his grandmother Julia, CAIUS JULIUS CAESAR OCTAVIANUS, accepted the title AUGUSTUS and used it as his praenomen in 27 B.C. after the nominal restoration of the Republic of Rome.) Born 63 B.C., he was studying at Apollonia in Illyria with Agrippa when Julius Caesar was assassinated in 44 and he learned that Caesar had adopted him and made him his heir, an appointment which was not officially recognised until the support of Caesar's troops gained him the consulship in 43. He then formed the triumvirate with Antony and Lepidus, defeated Brutus and Cassius at Philippi in 42, came to terms with Antony in 40, defeated Pompey in 36, and tried to restore peace in Italy after the warring years, though the threat remained in the east. In 32 he declared war on Cleopatra (not on Antony, whom the Senate had formally deprived of office), emerged as victor after Actium in 31 and Alexandria in 30, and celebrated his triumph in Rome in 29. In 27 he was Imperator, Augustus, consul, princeps but not king though in the provinces sometimes an official god, and from 23 he completely controlled the State by the power of veto although he declined to be styled dictator. Many of the following years were spent in pacifying and establishing the administration of the empire – he spent three continuous years in Gaul – but he was active in promoting domestic and moral legislation and in encouraging the cultural glories of Augustan Rome, and he was preoccupied for the last 40 years of his long life with the problem of who should succeed him. He had no son: his first wife bore him only a daughter, Julia, and his second wife, Livia, bore him no children though she had a son, Tiberius, by a former marriage whom she did not fail to champion. One by one the young men groomed by Augustus to succeed him died, sometimes in mysterious circumstances. They included two sons of Julia fathered by Augustus' old friend Agrippa, whom he had married to Julia as her second husband. Then Agrippa died. A decision was made that Julia should be married to Tiberius although he was already happily married. Eventually Augustus accepted Tiberius as his successor and co-administrator (though Tiberius avoided Rome and stayed with the armies). Augustus died in A.D. 14 and it was Livia who sent the urgent recall to Tiberius.

AULIS Harbour on the Euripus where the fleet of the Greeks assembled before sailing to Troy.

AURELIANUS (LUCIUS DOMITIUS AURELIANUS) A.D. 215–275, Roman emperor succeeding Claudius II in 270, extremely active militarily and as a reformer at home, but his severity cost him his life, taken by his staff officers as he prepared to march on Persia.

AURELIUS (commonly MARCUS AURELIUS, born MARCUS ANNIUS VERUS, after adoption MARCUS AELIUS AURELIUS VERUS CAESAR, reigned as emperor MARCUS AURELIUS ANTONINUS). Born A.D. 121, was very early picked out by the emperor Hadrian who subsequently adopted Antoninus Pius on condition that Antoninus adopted Marcus and another young prodigy, Lucius Verus, whose education he had also supervised. Marcus succeeded Antoninus as emperor in 161 and admitted Verus as partner, Verus mainly conducting successful military operations before he died in 169. Marcus had to take over a succession of wars and to institute much proxy administration, which may partially absolve him from responsibility for the persecution of the Christians from 177. He died 180 to achieve posthumous fame for his *Meditations* (extant), a pure expression of Stoic heathen philosophy.

[47]

AUSONIUS (DECIMUS MAGNUS AUSONIUS) An academic, A.D. 310–395, born in Burdigala (Bordeaux) but eventually governor of Gaul and consul in Rome, whose poems are in part extant.

AUSTER The south-west sirocco wind.

AUTOLYCUS Grandfather of Odysseus, excelled in thieving and swearing.

AUTOMEDON Charioteer and comrade of Achilles whose name, like Jehu's, was used for any charioteer.

AVENIO Modern Avignon.

AVERNUS LACUS A deep lake near Cumae in gloomy surroundings prompting the belief that it led to the underworld.

AVIANUS (FLAVIUS AVIANUS) *fl.* A.D. 400 wrote popular fables.

B

BABYLON Capital of ancient Mesopotamia built on both sides of the Euphrates, notable from 600 B.C.

BACCHAE 1. The Maenads, brutish women companions of Dionysus. 2. Frenzied priestesses of Dionysus.

BACCHYLIDES Lyric poet of Iulis in Ceos, *fl.* 5th century B.C.

BACTRIA Province of the Persian empire, modern Bokhara.

BAGOAS A eunuch of Artaxerxes III who died 336 B.C. His name was used to signify any eunuch.

BAIAE Coast town near Naples, the leisure resort of the Roman aristocracy.

BALEARES Two Mediterranean islands, Major and Minor, now Mallorca and Minorca.

BARCINO Modern Barcelona, a town of both Greek and Phoenician origin which became a Roman colonia.

BASILICA A Roman design for a public assembly hall or law court developed 184 B.C. – A.D. 350 which was adopted for Christian churches.

BATAVI A German tribe living on the Rhine delta based on Lug-

BELLEROPHON.

dunum (modern Leyden) accepted as Roman auxiliaries between 8 B.C. and A.D. 70.

BAVIUS A bad poet preserved in the amber of Virgil's *Eclogue* as Pope gave hacks an extension of life in the *Dunciad*.

BAUCIS An old countrywoman living with her husband Philemon. They were uniquely hospitable to Zeus and Hermes in Phrygia and the gods saved them from an inundation, gave them a shrine to serve in, and changed them into companion trees at their death.

BELGAE A formidably warlike people of German origin inhabiting Gaul north of the Sequana (modern Seine) and Matrona (modern Marne), some of them migrating to Britain, who resisted the conquest of Julius Caesar in both countries.

BELISARIUS Outstanding general of the emperor Justinian (ruled from Constantinople A.D. 527–565) who, relying mainly on cavalry, reconquered north Africa, 531, Sicily and Italy, 535–540. In 563 he was accused of conspiracy and the myth (probably untrue) is that he wandered through Constantinople as a blinded beggar. He died 565.

BELLEROPHON (BELLEROPHONTES) Son of Glaucus King of Corinth, grandson of Sisyphus, received his nickname after killing Bellerus, for which deed he sought purification from Proteus king of Argos. But Anteia, the queen, sexually rejected by Bellerophon, reported an attempted rape to her husband, who sent Bellerophon to Anteia's father, Iobates king of Lycia, asking him to kill him. Iobates deviously sent Bellerophon to kill the Chimaera, which he accomplished after taming the winged horse Pegasus, and later set him against an alliance of the Solymians and the Amazons, later against a pirate leader, and finally unsuccessfully ambushed him with his palace guard. Bellerophon's consistent victories convinced Iobates of his virtue, and he offered his daughter Philonoë in marriage. Later Bellerophon presumptuously decided to fly Pegasus to Olympus. Zeus sent a gadfly which stung the horse and Bellerophon was cast to earth.

BELLONA The Roman goddess of war, sister of Mars.

[51]

BELUS Son of Poseidon, father of Aegyptus and Danaus, reputed founder of Babylon by confusion with the god Baal.

BENACUS LACUS The modern Lake Garda.

BENDIS Thracian goddess associated with hunting and the moon.

BENEVENTUM Modern Benevento in south Italy, colonised in 268 B.C. by Romans who changed its name from Maleventum which it bore because of its foul air.

BERENICE 1. Name of a number of ladies in the family of the Ptolemies of Egypt, notably an elder sister of Cleopatra. 2. Sister of Herod the Great and mother of Agrippa I (Herod Agrippa). 3. Daughter of Agrippa I and mistress of her brother Agrippa II.

BERYTUS Modern Beirut, a city of Phoenicia.

BIBABULCULUS A Roman poet and lampoonist born 103 B.C.

BIBULUS (MARCUS CALPURNIUS BIBULUS) Colleague of Julius Caesar as aedile, 65 B.C., praetor, 62, and consul, 59 who later supported Pompey and died 48.

BION A cynical satirist in Athens c. 325–255 B.C.

BITHYNIA A district of north-west Asia Minor, became a province under Augustus.

BOCCHUS King of Mauretania, father-in-law of Jugurtha, died 33 B.C.

BOEOTIA District of central Greece north-west of Attica, long dominated by Thebes, home of Hesiod and Pindar.

BOETHIUS Roman statesman and author c. 480–524 A.D., wrote *De Consolatione Philosophiae* while imprisoned by Theodoric king of the Goths ruling from Rome.

BOII Celtic tribes whose principal migrations were to the Po valley around Bononia (modern Bologna), where they were subjugated 191 B.C., and to Boihemum (modern Bohemia), where they were exterminated 50 B.C.

BONA DEA A Roman goddess who revealed her oracles only to women.

BONONIA Modern Bologna, colonised by Rome 191 B.C.

BOOTES The constellation Arcturus.

BOREAS The north wind, friendly to Athens.

BOSPORUS The strait joining the Black Sea and the Mediterranean, named (literally as Ox-ford) because Io crossed it in the form of a heifer.

BOUDICCA Widow of the chieftain Prasutagas and queen of the Iceni in East Anglia, rebelled with the Trinovantes against Roman government and sacked London, but was defeated and killed herself A.D. 61.

BOULE The Council of 400 initiated at Athens by Solon.

BRANCHIDAE The site of the oracle of Apollo on the coast of Ionia south of Miletus containing relics of Ionic sculpture.

BRASIDAS Spartan general killed in battle against Cleon of Athens 422 B.C.

BRENNUS King of the Gauls who took and ransomed Rome in 390 B.C. and coined the phrase *Vae victis*.

BRIGANTES Powerful tribe of northern England based on Eburacum (modern York), conquered in A.D. 77.

BRISEIS The widow allotted as concubine to Achilles and claimed by Agamemnon.

BRITANNIA The island of England, Wales and Scotland, invaded by Julius Caesar 55 and 54 B.C., subdued as far north as the Forth and Clyde

A.D. 43–84, when the untamed north was named Caledonia, abandoned by the Romans in A.D. 407.

BRUTUS A Roman family of the Junia gens, named because the founder had to feign idiocy to survive Tarquin, and including: 1. LUCIUS JUNIUS BRUTUS nephew of Tarquinius Superbus, who expelled the Tarquins after the rape of Lucretia and as the founding consul of the republic killed his sons when they attempted to restore the Tarquins. 2. MARCUS JUNIUS BRUTUS 85–42 B.C., joined Pompey in the civil war against Julius Caesar in 49, was pardoned after the defeat of Pharsalus in 48, was active in the assassination of Caesar in 44, conducted successful military campaigns for the Senate in the next two years, joined Cassius against Antony and Octavian and committed suicide after the defeat at Philippi in 42.

BUBASTIS City in Lower Egypt where the cat-headed goddess Bubastis (Bast) was worshipped.

BUCEPHELAS The favourite horse of Alexander the Great which died at the end of his campaigns in 326 B.C. at a place in northern India where Alexander built the town Bucephala (modern Jhelum).

BURDIGALA A town in Aquitania, modern Bordeaux.

BUSIRIS Son of Poseidon, a king in Egypt who sacrificed all foreigners to Zeus but was killed by Heracles.

BYBLIS Nymph infatuated by her brother Caunus, finally changed into a fountain.

BYBLUS Town on the coast of Phoenicia, centre of the worship of Adonis.

BYZANTIUM Founded on the Thracian Bosporus by colonists from Megara on the isthmus of Corinth in 667 B.C., recolonised in 628. This settlement was wiped out by the Persians of Darius I, but the site was captured and recolonised with a mixed force of Spartans and Athenians by Pausanias of Sparta after the battle of Plataea in 479, and Athens and

Sparta disputed its sovereignty through the fifth century B.C. It was besieged by Philip of Macedon in 340, but was preserved through a miraculous flash of light which revealed the approaching army and which it perpetuated on its coinage as a Crescent, still used by the Turks. It resisted attacks by the Thracian Gauls and did not come under Roman rule until the emperor Septimius Severus razed it and rebuilt it in A.D. 196. Constantine made it his capital and re-named it Constantinople in A.D. 330. It fell to the Moslems in 1453 and gradually extended the use of its Turkish name, Istanbul (Stamboul).

C

CABIRI Phrygian deities of fertility adopted by Greek maritime communities especially as propitious to sailors.

CACUS Fire-breathing giant son of Hephaestus and Medusa who stole the cattle tended by Heracles and was consequently battered to death by the hero. (The Romans capitalised on the story, since the cave of Cacus was on Mount Aventine, and in their terminology he was the son of Vulcan confronted by Hercules.)

CADMUS Grandson of Poseidon, son of Agenor king of Tyre, and brother of Europa, whom Zeus in the guise of a gentle bull enticed away and subsequently raped. Cadmus and his brothers sailed separately to seek her, and Cadmus eventually founded the city of Thebes. He killed a dragon who was impeding his sacrifice to Athena and she told him to sow the dragon's teeth in the soil. Armed men sprang up, brawling and fighting until there remained only five, who were the original elders of Thebes. The nuptials of Cadmus and Harmonia, daughter of Aphrodite and Ares, was the first wedding of mortals attended by the Olympians, who sat on twelve thrones and brought legendary gifts. Cadmus introduced into Greece 'writing' – that is, the Phoenician or North Semitic alphabet of sixteen letters.

CADUCEUS The enchanter's wand (and herald's staff) carried by Hermes, both as the messenger of the gods and the intimator of death, by gently laying the golden rod on the eyes of the dying.

CAECILIUS (CAECILIUS STATUS) Roman comic playwright, died 168 B.C.

CAELIUS (MARCUS CAELIUS RUFUS) Roman orator of wit and invective who succeeded Catullus as the lover of Clodia and was defended by Cicero in an ensuing criminal charge. He rebelled against Julius Caesar and was executed 48 B.C.

CAENEUS Originally a Nymph, the bedmate of Poseidon who at her request changed her into a man with an invulnerable skin. He became king of the Lapiths and demanded worship as a god. At Zeus' instigation he was overcome by the Centaurs, who smothered him underground. The soul escaped as a bird. The body was found as a woman's corpse.

CAESAR The name of a patrician family of the gens Julia claiming descent from Aeneas; after the adoption of Augustus by Julius Caesar the term was an imperial title. CAIUS JULIUS CAESAR, born 102 B.C. (traditionally 100 B.C.) became politically out of favour in 83 and opted for military service in Asia. He returned to Rome in 78 and matured in skill and popularity as an advocate and administrator: quaestor 68, aedile 65, praetor 62, consul 59 when he formed a trium-virate with Pompey and Crassus and took over Transalpine and Cisalpine Gaul, eventually for ten years, an appointment which gave him an army. During this period he subjugated Gaul and twice invaded Britain but did not reduce the island. In 49 he was ordered by the Senate to relinquish his command, but he kept it, and crossed the Rubicon. He became master of Italy and Spain and, in 48, of Greece when he defeated Pompey at Pharsalus. He pursued Pompey to Egypt, where he installed as queen Cleopatra, already his mistress. In Rome he was appointed consul and dictator in 48, and in 44 the consulship was extended for his life, though he refused the title of king. He was assassinated in 44 B.C. as the result of a conspiracy headed by Brutus and Cassius. Most of his literary works, which critically were greatly admired, are lost and only his war com-mentaries remain.

CAESAREA (CAESAREA PALAESTINAE) Coastal town in Israel rebuilt by Herod the Great between 22 and 10 B.C. the king changing the name from Stratonis Turris and calling its splendid new harbour

Portus Augusti. It was the capital of (Roman) Judaea and the residence of the procurator, St Paul being imprisoned there for two years. The Jews in its population were massacred in A.D. 66.

CAESARION The son of Cleopatra by Julius Caesar, born 47 B.C. and formally named Ptolemaeus, executed by Augustus in 30 B.C. as a threat to the succession.

CAESTUS The boxing-'glove' of the Romans, more strictly a knuckle-duster, a leather strap embossed with metal and wound round the hands.

CALCHAS Skilful soothsayer of the Greeks at Troy who died at Claros of mortification (or, some say, laughter) when he met Mopsus an even more precise diviner.

CALE Modern Oporto.

CALEDONIA The modern Scottish Highlands, land of the Caledonii, defeated but not subdued by Agricola at Mons Graupius in A.D. 84, punitively pacified by the emperor Septimius Severus in 209, but so briefly that they contributed to the despair in which Severus died at York in A.D. 211.

CALENDS The first day of the Roman month.

CALIGULA (CAIUS JULIUS CAESAR GERMANICUS) Known in his time as Caius Caesar, Caligula being a soldiers' nickname derived from the miniature military boots (caligae) he wore as a child when sharing his father's life as a soldier. The son of Germanicus and Agrippina, born in A.D. 12, he was groomed for the succession by Tiberius and succeeded him as emperor in 37. After a fair beginning he became mentally unbalanced, megalomaniac to the point of self-deification, licentious to the extreme of incest with his sister Drusilla, wildly extravagant and inhumanly cruel. He was assassinated in 41 with his fourth wife, Caesonia, and his only child.

CALLICRATES Greek architect of the 5th century B.C. who built the Parthenon with Ictinus and Phidias.

CALLIMACHUS 1. Greek sculptor, *fl.* after 450 B.C., the first to use the running-drill for the decoration of marble and said to be the inventor of the Corinthian capital in architecture. 2. Poet and grammarian, keeper of the library at Alexandria from 260 B.C. until he died in 240.

CALLIOPE Muse, mother of Orpheus and goddess of epic poetry.

CALLISTHENES Nephew and pupil of Aristotle, *c.* 360–328 B.C., executed by Alexander the Great for *lèse-majesté*.

CALLISTO Nymph from Arcadia, mother by Zeus of Arcas (whence Arcadia), transformed by Zeus into a she-bear to conceal this liaison from Hera, but the stratagem failed and Hera caused Artemis to shoot Callisto while hunting. Zeus transformed her into the constellations of the Bear, Arctos.

CALLISTRATUS The name under which Aristophanes wrote his first three plays.

CALPE The rock of Gibraltar.

CALPURNIA The last wife of Julius Caesar whom she married in 59 B.C., notably attached to him in spite of his liaison with Cleopatra and his previous wish to remarry his second wife, Pompeia, the woman he had divorced in 61 because 'Caesar's wife must be above suspicion'.

CALPURNIUS (TITUS CALPURNIUS SICULUS) Roman pastoral poet who flourished *c.* A.D. 50.

CALYDON Town in Aetolia, north of the western stretch of the gulf of Corinth, in the mountains where the hunt for the Calydonian boar took place.

CALYPSO Nymph, daughter of Atlas, living on the island of Ogygia. Odysseus was shipwrecked there after escaping from Circe. Calypso promised him immortality if he would remain with her but she released him after seven years.

CAMBYSES 1. Father of Cyrus the Great. 2. Son of Cyrus the Great, reigned 529–521 B.C., conquered Egypt 525, developed into a murderous tyrant.

CAMENAE Roman water-nymphs.

CAMILLA Daughter of king Metabus of Privernum of the Volsci, who to preserve her tied her to a javelin, dedicated her to Diana and threw her across the river Amisenus. She aided Turnus against Aeneas and was killed by Arruns.

CAMILLUS (MARCUS FURIUS CAMILLUS) Roman censor 403 B.C. and on five occasions later appointed dictator in times of imminent extinction by the Gauls, notably after Brennus took the capital in 390. Termed the second Romulus, he died in 365 aged 82.

CAMPANIA The fertile area south of Latium and embracing Naples.

CAMPUS MARTIUS Plain in a bend of the Tiber outside the city walls where the Roman youth practised gymnastic and military exercises and the assembly known as the COMITIA CENTURIATA was held. Augustus built it up ostentatiously and Aurelian enclosed it within the city.

CAMULODUNUM Modern Colchester, former capital of the Trinobantes, later the first Roman colony in Britain, founded by Claudius in A.D. 43.

CANDACE The name of all queens of Aethiopia, notably the queen defeated by Petronius when invading Roman Egypt in 22 B.C.

CANIDIA Horace's pseudonym for the courtesan of Naples who jilted him and whom he later pilloried.

CANNAE A village on the river Aufidus in Apulia where Hannibal defeated the Romans in 216 B.C.

CANOPUS A prosperous coastal town near Alexandria famous for its licence and its temple of Serapis.

CANUSIUM Grecian town in Apulia, modern Canosa.

CAPANEUS One of the heroic Seven who marched against Thebes, destroyed on the ramparts by a thunderbolt from Zeus.

CAPITOL (CAPITOLIUM, MONS CAPITOLINUS) The temple of Jupiter Optimus Maximus, eventually flanked by shrines to Juno and Minerva, a majestic building to which Roman generals were carried during their triumph and where the Sibylline books were kept.

CAPPADOCIA A region of Asia Minor, the boundaries of which differed at various times. A Roman province from A.D. 17.

CAPREAE The island, modern Capri, where Tiberius spent his last ten years in debauchery.

CAPUA The principal city of Campania, an Etruscan foundation c. 600 B.C., emasculated in power on recovery by the Romans after it revolted to Hannibal in 216 B.C.

CAPYS Father of Anchises.

CARACALLA (MARCUS AURELIUS ANTONINUS) A.D. 188–217. Son of Septimius Severus, on whose death he made peace with the Caledonians, murdered his brother, and ruled as Roman emperor from 211.

CARATACUS Leader of the south-east British Resistance to the Romans, after the fall of Camulodunum in A.D. 43, rallied the western British, defeated near the present Welsh border he escaped to the Brigantes in modern Yorkshire whose queen, Cartimandua, sold him to the Romans in 51. Claudius spared his life in Rome when he made an impressive speech in justification.

CARALIS Modern Cagliari in Sardinia.

CARIA The fertile south-western corner of Asia Minor, earlier settled by Greek colonists, later part of Roman Asia, of which the principal city was Halicarnassus.

CARINUS (MARCUS AURELIUS CARINUS) Elder son of CARUS, whom see, and left by him as Caesar of the West when Carus marched against Persia; formal emperor A.D. 284–285, assassinated for sexual revenge while winning a battle against Diocletian.

CARNA A Roman goddess of physical fitness.

CARNEA A Spartan festival of Apollo adapted from previous worship of a ram-god.

CARNEADES Sceptic philosopher 213–129 B.C. who founded the Third Academy in Athens, opposed the Stoics, and was highly thought of in Rome, which he visited.

CARNUNTUM Ancient Celtic settlement on the Danube east of Vindobona (modern Vienna) which became a key Roman fortress, headquarters of the XV Legion for a century from A.D. 16.

CARPATES The (Carpathian) mountains between Dacia and Sarmatia.

CARTHAGE(MAGNA CARTHAGO) City north-east of modern Tunis traditionally founded by Phoenicians from Tyre in 9th century B.C. and maintaining its strength through an efficient oligarchy and a mercenary army. The Carthaginians became imperialist rivals of the Romans and the Punic wars successively stripped them of Sicily, (265–242 B.C.), sapped their resources to exhaustion (218–201 B.C.), and brought the entire destruction of their capital (146 B.C.). The new Colonia Carthago became important as a commercial and ecclesiastical centre. It was in the hands of the Vandals A.D. 439–533 and was destroyed by the Arabs A.D. 698.

CARTHAGO NOVA Port in Spain with magnificent harbour, modern Cartagena, founded by Hasdrubal in 228 B.C., a Roman colony subsequently, destroyed by the Vandals A.D. 425.

CARUS (MARCUS AURELIUS CARUS) Promoted himself emperor in A.D. 282, left his son Carinus to keep the West and took his second son Numerian east against the Danube tribes and eventually

Persia, where he died at the end of 283, probably assassinated, officially struck by a thunderbolt.

CARYATIDES Columns of Greek buildings carved as women, as in the Erectheum on the Athenian Acropolis, named after the town of Caryae in Laconia near Arcadia, whose women were put into rigorous slavery when the city allied itself with the Persians invading Greece.

CASSANDER Son of Antipater (1), had to initiate vigorous intrigue and action before he succeeded his father as ruler of Macedonia 319-297 B.C.

CASSANDRA Beautiful daughter of Priam and Hecuba of Troy and sister of Helenus, given the talent of prophecy by Apollo as bribery for her future favours, which she then teasingly denied and the god added the condition that she would never be believed. At the sack of Troy she was raped by Ajax the Lesser and was part of the prize of Agamemnon, whose wife killed her.

CASSIODORUS (FLAVIUS MAGNUS AURELIUS CASSIODORUS) c. A.D. 490-583, Roman statesman and author, an authority on the history of the Gothic kingdom of Rome.

CASSIOPEIA (CASSIOPE) Mother of Andromeda who boasted of her daughter's beauty and was in ridicule placed as a constellation revolving apparently upside down.

CASSITERIDES The name 'Tin Islands' applied loosely to Britain and Ireland, and specifically to Cornwall and the Scillies.

CASSIUS The name of a gens in Rome among whose members was CAIUS CASSIUS LONGINUS, a distinguished soldier who became a tribune in 49, supported Pompey's revolt but accepted a pardon from Julius Caesar after the battle of Pharsalus in Thessaly, 48 B.C. He led the conspiracy of 44 against Caesar, claimed and plundered Syria as his reward after the assassination, was defeated by Antony at Philippi (though his ally Brutus beat Octavian) and committed suicide, 42 B.C.

CASSIVELLAUNUS Local king in modern Hertfordshire made commander-in-chief of the British forces opposing Caesar's invasion of Britain, 54 B.C.

CASTOR One of the Dioscuri, a heroic son of Zeus with his twin Polydeuces (Pollux to the Romans), yet not in reality a son of Zeus but the offspring of Tyndareus king of Sparta by his daughter Leda who was almost simultaneously impregnated by Zeus, and accordingly bore at the same birth the mortal Castor and the divine Polydeuces – an elaborate manufacture of a myth to rationalise the primitive institution of a sacred king reigning with a lay king. These devoted twins marched against Athens to rescue their sister Helen who had been carried off by Theseus; sailed with the Argonauts, when Polydeuces outboxed Amycus; and battled with the twins Idas and Lynceus, a fight in which Castor, the mortal man of the pair, died. Polydeuces prayed that he, though immortal, should not outlive his brother, and Zeus in mercy let them live on alternate days and later placed them in the firmament as the stars called the Heavenly Twins. The two were particularly worshipped at Sparta and among the Romans.

CATANA A Greek colony founded at the foot of Aetna by settlers from Naxos in 729 B.C. and after many vicissitudes made a Roman colonia under Augustus. (Modern Catania.)

CATARRHACTES A river in Pamphylia in Asia Minor descending from the Taurus mountains in a broken waterfall.

CATALINE (LUCIUS SERGIUS CATALINA) After a rebellious and vicious youth became governor of Africa 68–66 B.C. After later acquittal on a charge of extortion he headed a conspiracy against the State in 63 which was put down by Cicero as consul, and Cataline was defeated and died in battle in 62.

CATO The name of members of a Roman family of the gens Porcia, notably MARCUS PORCIUS CATO the Censor, 234–149 B.C., left his father's farm for long military service ending at Thermopylae in 191 B.C. He entered politics as a puritan reformer, and as censor in 184 he heavily taxed luxuries and spent the money on sewers. He was later responsible for many conservative measures and for the propaganda *delenda est Carthago* which led to the Third Punic War.

CATULLUS (CAIUS VALERIUS CATULLUS) Lyric poet and satirist, *c.* 84–54 B.C., born in Verona and came in 62 to Rome where he became infatuated with Clodia, his 'Lesbia'.

CAUDIUM A town between Beneventum and Capua near which was the pass called the Caudine Forks, where the Roman army surrendered to the Samnites in 321 B.C. and was ceremonially sent under the yoke.

CEBES Philosopher from Thebes, friend and pupil of Socrates who was present at his death, 399 B.C.

CECROPS Mythical first king of Attica, the gift of Athena. He founded Athens and instituted monogamy and religious worship without blood sacrifice.

CELAENO One of the three Harpies (Harpyiae) the ghostly snatchers.

CELEUS King of Eleusis who received Demeter when she was seeking Core (Persephone), but Demeter off-handedly turned his son Abas into a lizard and fumbled the operation intended to immortalise another son, Demophoön, so that he died. Celeus became first priest of Demeter at Eleusis.

CELTS A strongly characterised race, variously called by the ancients Celtae, Galatae and Galli, which for five centuries after 900 B.C. dominated non-Mediterranean Europe from Finsterre to the Bosporus (even founding the state of Galatia in Asia Minor). Gradually assimilated or conquered, their highly distinctive art and religion was most strongly preserved in Ireland and western Britain.

CENSOR One of the Roman officials charged with conducting the census of persons and property and with the supervision of morals.

CENTAURS Wild monsters, generally pictured as a combination of man and horse, dwelling on Mount Pelion in Thessaly, having an inherent primitive attraction on account of their 'human' lusts for wine and sexuality. They fought the Lapiths when invited to the marriage feast of Peirithous king of that people, and they once attacked Heracles. Chiron, often called king of the Centaurs, was by comparison mild and cultured.

CENTUMVIRI A court of justice providing a jury picked from 100 men in Rome, concerned with civil actions and particularly disputes over inheritance.

CEPHALUS A timid adulterer, desired by Eos, the amorous goddess of dawn. Cephalus refused her advances pleading a vow of faithfulness between him and his wife Procris. Eos declared that Procris would speedily lose her virtue if the price was right, and changed the appearance of Cephalus, who, in the guise of a stranger, offered a gold crown to Procris, successfully occupied her bed, and smugly left it for that of Eos. Meanwhile Procris surrendered to Minos for the reward of a hound that never missed its quarry and a javelin that never missed its mark. She returned with these to Cephalus but she maintained a disguise as a youth. Cephalus coveted her magic possessions, and Procris, still apparently a youth, said Cephalus could only procure them by taking their owner to bed. Cephalus did this, and Procris revealed herself as his wife. Later, still mutually jealous, Procris was accidentally killed by Cephalus with the unfailing javelin.

CEPHISSUS (CEPHISUS) The name of several rivers in Greece, notably that in Boeotia falling into lake Copais, and the largest river in Attica, flowing past Athens and flowing into the Saronic gulf near Phalerum.

CERBERUS Many-headed dog guarding the gates of Hades.

CERES An Italian corn-goddess who was given many of the attributes of Demeter.

CEYX The husband of ALCYONE, whom see.

CHABRIAS A soldier of Athens, inventor of an effective tactical defence manouevre, who fought as a mercenary general for Cyprus and Egypt and died at the siege of Chios, 357 B.C.

CENTAUR.

CHIRON.

CHAERONEA Town on the Boeotian Cephissus where Philip defeated the Athenians and Thebans, extinguishing Grecian liberty, in 338 B.C., and Sulla beat Mithridates' general Archelaus in 86 B.C.

CHALCIDICE The three-pronged peninsula in Macedonia founded from Chalcis.

CHALDAEA A province of Babylon at the head of the Persian gulf, later used to signify all the State of Babylon.

CHALYBES An Asian people famous for working iron mines on the south-east coast of the Black Sea.

CHAOS A gaping void which was the first Creation and from which the world of gods and men developed.

CHARES A controversial Athenian general, *fl.* 366–322 B.C.

CHARITES The Graces: goddesses of charm and beauty, Euphrosyne, (Joy), Aglaia (Radiant) and Thalia (the Flowering).

CHARON Aged ferryman, son of Erebos the dark god, who carried the shades of the dead across the rivers of the lower world for the fee of an obolus, a coin placed in the mouth of the dead.

CHARYBDIS The whirlpool opposite the cave of Scylla, perilous to mariners, modern identification on the west side of the strait of Messina.

CHERSONESUS The Thracian Chersonesus is the Gallipoli peninsula of the Dardanelles, the Tauric Chersonesus is the Crimea.

CHERUSCI A powerful German tribe living between the Harz and the Elbe but principally based on the Weser.

CHIMAERA A fire-breathing monster with the head of a lion, the behind of a dragon and the middle of a goat, killed by Bellerophon.

CHIOS Fertile and intellectually cultured Aegean island off Ionia, the birthplace of Homer.

CHIRON The gentlest and wisest of the Centaurs who instructed many heroes of the Grecian tradition in the arts of healing, hunting, music and prophecy. He gave up his immortality to Prometheus, and was placed among the stars as Sagittarius.

CHLORIS 1. The goddess of Spring. 2. The only daughter of Niobe who was not killed. 3. The mother of Nestor.

CHOERILUS 1. Athenian tragic playwright writing from 523 B.C. 2. Epic poet from Samos, formerly regarded as in Homer's class, a friend of Herodotus. 3. A notably bad epic poet from Iasus, paid to flatter Alexander the Great at the rate of one gold stater per line.

CHORUS The company who sang and danced at Greek religious festivals.

CHRYSEIS Daughter of Chryses, the priest of Apollo at Chryse who was taken prisoner during the siege of Troy and passed to Agamemnon as a prize. Chryses came to beg her freedom but his offer of a ransom was refused. Apollo therefore visited the camp of the Greeks with pestilence which was to last until the girl was handed back. When Agamemnon finally did this he claimed Briseis from Achilles and began the celebrated quarrel in the *Iliad*.

CHRYSIPPUS A Stoic philosopher, 280–207 B.C., born in Cilicia but worked mainly in Athens and was a very prolific writer.

CICERO (MARCUS TULLIUS CICERO) Roman orator, statesman and philosopher, 106–43 B.C., began pleading as an advocate 81, quaestor in Sicily 75, praetor 66, consul 63 when he suppressed the Cataline conspiracy, spent two periods in Greece, one under political banishment 58, appointed legate to Julius Caesar but later sided with Pompey in the civil war of 49, pardoned by Caesar 48. On the assassination of Caesar in 44 he assumed leadership of the republican party and bitterly attacked Mark Antony. He was consequently executed on the orders of the triumvirate in 43.

CILICIA An area in south-east Asia Minor said to have been settled by Cilix who halted in his search for his sister Europa.

CIMBRI A Celtic people originally inhabiting Jutland who campaigned vigorously against the Romans for a quarter-century until they were annihilated at Campi Raudii near modern Verona in 101 B.C.

CIMMERII 1. A mythical people dwelling on the border of the western ocean. 2. A Caucasian people who penetrated into Asia Minor but were expelled in the 7th century B.C.

CIMON c. 512–449 B.C., a vigorous general of the Athenian fleets, son of Miltiades.

CINARA Aegean island renowned for artichokes.

CINCINNATUS (TITUS QUINCTIUS CINCINNATUS) Traditional Roman hero and model of humility who was called from his plough in 458 B.C. to serve as dictator and, after taking over the army to defeat the Aequi, returned to his farm after 16 days. He died after 439 B.C.

CINEAS Thessalian diplomatist who made a famous embassage to Rome for Pyrrhus king of Epirus in 280 B.C.

CINGETORIX A pro-Roman Gallic leader of the city of Treviri (modern Tréves).

CINNA (LUCIUS CORNELIUS CINNA) Consul in Rome 87–84 B.C., leading the movement against Sulla.

CINYRAS Son of Apollo, king of Cyprus and founder of the cult of the Paphian Aphrodite which practised sacred prostitution, father of Adonis through involuntary incest with his daughter Myrrha (Smyrna).

CIRCE Daughter of Helios who detained Odysseus with her enchantment on the island of Aeaea and became by him the mother of Telegonus.

CIRCUS MAXIMUS In Rome the course for chariot-racing and military reviews.

CITHAERON The mountain range between Attica and Boeotia sacred to Dionysus and the Muses, site of the death of Actaeon.

CITIUM A town in Cyprus where Cimon died and Zeno was born.

CLAROS Ancient sanctuary near Colophon with an oracle of Apollo.

CLAUDIA QUINTA A Roman matron who cleared herself of a charge of adultery in 204 B.C. by hauling a ship stranded in the Tiber and containing an image of Cybele, which the diviners said could be refloated only by a chaste woman.

CLAUDIAN (CLAUDIUS CLAUDIANUS) An Alexandrian known to have lived in Milan and Rome A.D. 395–404, the author of a number of extant poems and panegyrics.

CLAUDIUS (TIBERIUS CLAUDIUS DRUSUS NERO GERMANICUS) 10 B.C. – A.D. 54 was the youngest son of Tiberius' brother Drusus, was barred by physical handicaps from public office, but after the murder of Caligula was proclaimed emperor by the Praetorian Guard in order to foil the purpose of the Senate, then sitting, to declare a republic, A.D. 41. He executed his third wife, the notorious Messalina, in 48, only to exchange her for his niece Agrippina, who eventually poisoned him in 54 to secure the succession of her son Britannicus. In Britain he was present at the capture of Camulodunum in 43.

CLAUDIUS, (APPIUS CLAUDIUS) Roman statesman and writer, consul 307 and 296 B.C., an aristocrat who brought in the plebs to a newly-shaped democracy.

CLAUDIUS (MARCUS AURELIUS CLAUDIUS GOTHICUS) was an officer of Gallienus chosen to succeed him as emperor in A.D. 268, decisively defeated the Goths and died 270.

HERCULES AND CERBERUS.

CLEANTHES A Stoic philosopher and disciple of Zeno who practised philosophy for 19 years, supporting himself by work at night in drawing water, *c.* 300–220 B.C.

CLEARCHUS A Spartan general *c.* 450–401 B.C. who later served Cyrus as a mercenary.

CLEOBULUS One of the seven sages of Lindos in Rhodes *c.* 580 B.C., particularly adept at riddles.

CLEOMBRUTUS 1. The name of a number of kings of Sparta. 2. A philosopher who killed himself after reading Plato, in order to find a better life.

CLEOMENES 1. The name of three kings of Sparta. 2. An Athenian sculptor who carved the Venus di Medici.

CLEON An Athenian politician, son of a tanner, opponent of Pericles until his death in 429 B.C., a successful operator though presented as a vulgar demagogue.

CLEOPATRA 1. The name of the queens of Ptolemy V, VI and VIII. 2. The beautiful daughter of Ptolemy XI (Auletes) and Ptolemy's sister Cleopatra V (Tryphaena), born *c.* 70 B.C. of purely Macedonian blood, became Julius Caesar's mistress in 48 and followed him to Rome, leaving after his death, becoming the mistress of Mark Antony in Alexandria 41–40 B.C. and celebrating a marriage with him in 37, when he installed her as queen of Egypt. After defeat by Octavian at Actium and Octavian's seizure of her at Alexandria in 30 she committed suicide with an asp as the instrument of her god.

CLIMAX The name of the western end of the Taurus mountain range in south-east Asia Minor.

CLIO The muse of history.

CLITOR A town in the north of Arcadia with a fountain the waters of which were said to impart a distaste for wine.

CLITUMNUS A river in Umbria the waters of which eventually ran into the Tiber.

CLITUS A Macedonian general and friend of Alexander the Great, killed by Alexander in the drunken heat of a banquet.

CLODIA A profligate Roman aristocrat, the mistress of Catullus, who called her Lesbia in his poems.

CLOELIA A Roman virgin delivered as a hostage to Porsena of the Etruscans, who escaped by swimming the Tiber, was delivered back to Porsena, but was freed in admiration for her deed and had an equestrian statue erected to her in Rome.

CLOTHO One of the Fates, she who span the web.

CLUSIUM The seat, and later the mausoleum, of Porsena of the Etruscans, modern Chiusi.

CLYMENE 1. Daughter of Oceanus and Tethys, wife of Iapetus, mother of Atlas and Prometheus. 2. Mother of Phaethon by Hellos though she was the wife of Merops, king of Aethiopia.

CLYTAEMNESTRA The daughter of Tyndareus and Leda, sister of Castor and Polydeuces and Helen, wife of Agamemnon and mother of Orestes, Iphigenia and Electra. During the Trojan war she lived in adultery with Aegisthus, and murdered Agamemnon on his return. She was put to death by Orestes.

CNIDUS A Greek colony in Caria, Asia Minor, where the statue of Aphrodite by Praxiteles was displayed.

CNSOSOS The ancient capital of king Minos of Crete, known by archaelogical findings to date from the Neolithic Age in the fourth millennium B.C.

COCALUS The king of Sicily who welcomed Daedalus after his flight from Crete and connived at the subsequent murder of Minos.

COCYTUS A river in Epirus supposed to lead to the lower world.

CODRUS The last king of Athens who sacrificed himself to save the city from the Dorians.

COLCHIS An area of Asia east of the Black Sea and south of the Caucasus, the destination of Jason.

COLONIA AGRIPPINENSIS Colony founded in A.D. 50 by Claudius in honour of his wife Agrippina, who was born there: modern Cologne.

COLONUS A hill near the Academy in Athens, the birthplace of Sophocles and grave of Oedipus, having a temple to Poseidon.

COLOSSAE A city of Phrygia to the inhabitants of which St Paul wrote his epistle.

COLOSSEUM The Amphitheatrum Flavianum at Rome, holding 45,000 spectators, finished by Titus in A.D. 80.

COMITIUM An assembly and law court in Rome later incorporated into the Forum.

COMMIUS A Gallic king of the Atrebates appointed by Caesar and sent by him to Britain for the invasion. But he revolted in Gaul in 52 B.C. and later founded a dynasty in Britain.

COMMODUS (LUCIUS AELIUS AURELIUS COMMODUS) Roman emperor A.D. 180–192. Strangled by an athlete when the poison administered to him by his mistress worked too slowly.

COMUM Birthplace of the elder and the younger Pliny, modern Como.

COMUS A comparatively modern god of mirth.

CONCORDIA The Roman goddess of concord, had a temple near the Forum.

CONFLUENTES The town at the junction of the Moselle and the Rhine, modern Coblentz.

CONSENTES DI The twelve principle Roman gods, derived via the Etruscans from Olympia, whose statues, six male and six female, stood in the Forum.

CONSTANS Youngest son of Constantine the Great who inherited Illyricum, Italy and Africa on his father's death in A.D. 337 but subsequently became emperor of the West.

CONSTANTINE (FLAVIUS VALERIUS CONSTANTINUS) *c.* A.D. 274–337, was heir to the emperor Constantius Chlorus (ruled 305–306) who died at York, and he was proclaimed emperor by the troops there. Amid dynastic confusion he announced the formation of a new imperial house in 310 and conquered Rome in 312, later granting extensive favours to the Christians. He fought and defeated Licinius for the empire of the East, moved to Byzantium and re-dedicated it as Constantinopolis in 330. He was baptised shortly before his death in 337. He was succeeded as Roman emperor by his son Constantinus II who ruled A.D. 337–340.

CONSUS A Roman god, originally of the harvest, later identified with Poseidon.

COPAIS The lake in Boeotia formed by the waters of the Cephissus.

CORAX Sicilian from Syracuse who wrote the first work on the art and practice of rhetoric, *c.* 467 B.C.

CORCYRA Island colonised from Corinth in the 7th century B.C. and later a maritime rival of that city. Modern Corfu.

CORDUBA Spanish city, later a Roman colonia, the birthplace of Lucan and the two Senecas, modern Cordoba.

CORE Demeter's straying daughter, later called Persephone.

CORINNA A woman poet of Tanagra in Boeotia, said to have triumphed over Pindar at a public contest.

CORINTH (CORINTHUS) The isthmus city which exploited its two ports to become the commercial and maritime leader in Greece, destroyed by the Romans in 146 B.C., but rebuilt and re-peopled under Julius Caesar.

CORIOLANUS (CNAEUS MARCIUS CORIOLANUS) was a legendary Roman hero who withdrew from Rome when charged with tyrannously opposing the plebs, and led an army of the Volscii against the city in 491 B.C. He spared Rome on the entreaties of his wife Volumnia and his mother Veturia, and was executed by the Volscians.

CORIOLI Latian capital of the Volscii which the above Coriolanus captured in 493 B.C.

CORNELIA *Fl.* mid-2nd century B.C., a Roman matron who became idolised as the Mother of the Gracchi, Tiberius and Caius Gracchus.

CORNELIUS NEPOS An author and the friend of Cicero, *c.* 99–24 B.C., originator of extant biographies.

CORONIS Mother of Asclepius by Apollo, who left a white crow to guard her through pregnancy, but she kept company with Ischys. The crow flew swiftly back to Delphi to report this, but Apollo knew already, and cursed the crow for not pecking out the eyes of Ischys, and the crow turned black. Artemis shot Coronis dead with arrows in sympathy for Apollo, but he in remorse snatched her body from the funeral pyre and beckoned to Hermes to cut Asclepius, who was still living, from her womb.

CORSICA Colonised from Phocaea in Asia Minor about 565 B.C., but taken by Carthaginians in 565. Rome took it during the first Punic war but with the fall of the empire it passed to Vandals, Goths and Saracens.

CORVUS (MARCUS VALERIUS CORVUS) Given the cognomen because a raven helped him to defeat a Gaul in single combat by flapping in his enemy's face, six times consul in Rome and twice dictator between 348 and 299 B.C., and traditionally lived to be 100 years old.

CORYBANTES Priests of Cybele (in Phrygia), Rhea in Crete, and Attis who danced to the drum and cymbal.

COS One of the islands of the Sporades, off Caria in Asia Minor, where Hippocrates pioneered medicine, famous later for the production of diaphanous dresses.

COSSUS (AULUS CORNELIUS COSSUS) Consul in Rome in 428 B.C., when he won the very rare *spolia opima* granted to a general after single combat with an enemy, killing Lars Tolumnius of Veii.

COTHURNUS The buskins worn by Greek tragic actors to add to their height.

CRASSUS (MARCUS LICINIUS CRASSUS, called DIVES) Roman capitalist, speculator and general, *c.* 112–53 B.C., devoted most of his life to the successful pursuit of riches, overcame Spartacus in 71, bought Julius Caesar in 65, and formed the triumvirate with him and Pompey in 60, took the military governorship of Syria in 55 intending to make a further fortune, but was defeated by the Parthians at Carrhae in Mesopotamia and shortly afterwards treacherously killed. His head was sent to Orodes king of Parthia, who poured molten gold into the mouth with the invitation 'Drink your fill!'

CRATERUS Macedonian general, *c.* 370–321 B.C. who was sent back from the East by Alexander the Great to take over Macedonia and Greece but fell in his first battle.

CRATES Athenian comic playwright *fl.* 470–450 B.C.

CRATINUS An admitted drunkard, 519–422 B.C., acknowledged even by Aristophanes to have been a masterly comic dramatist.

CREON King of Corinth whose daughter, Glauce, was married to Jason and therefore incinerated by Medea, Creon himself dying in the conflagration.

CRONUS AND RHEA.

CRETE (CRETA, CANDIA) Island populated in prehistoric times, settled by Dorians around 1000 B.C., remained a fertile and prosperous island mainly outside the Grecian orbit, though constantly of strategic importance, finally assimilated as a province of Rome under Augustus.

CRITIAS One of the 30 Tyrants set up in Athens by the Spartans in 404 B.C., a cruel and greedy man, honoured, however, by his kinsman Plato for his intellectual talent. He was killed in 403.

CRITO (CRITON) A wealthy Athenian devoted to Socrates.

CROCUS A youth in love with another called Smilax, and changed into the saffron plant.

CROESUS The last king of Lydia, c. 560 B.C., overthrown by Cyrus of Persia, 546 B.C. His fabulous wealth attracted to his court at Sardis, among other philosophers, Solon, who said 'Call no man happy until he has died happy.' Remembering this at the stake where he was condemned to be burned to death, Croesus called out 'Solon! Solon! Solon!' Cyrus asked the reason, spared his life, and made him his friend and ally.

CRONUS The Titan son of Uranus and Mother Earth who cast his father down and was in turn deposed by Zeus, whom he sired on Rhea with Poseidon, Hades, Hera, Demeter and Hestia.

CROTON A powerful city in Magna Graecia on the toe of Italy.

CTESIAS A Greek physician to Artaxerxes, used as an envoy in 398 B.C. and the author of a history of Persia.

CUMAE Port near Naples, the earliest Greek colony, settled from Chalcis in A.D. 750, the reputed landing place of Daedalus after his flight from Crete, a great colonising power in its own turn and the site of the oracle of the Sybil.

CURIA 1. An early administrative division of the Romans, according to family or neighbourhood. 2. An assembly house of such a gathering, particularly the Senate house of Rome.

CURTIUS (QUINTUS CURTIUS RUFUS) Roman historian of Alexander the Great, writing c. A.D. 50.

CYBELE The Anatolian mother-goddess later associated with the Greek Demeter.

CYCLADES The Aegean islands circling Delos.

CYCLOPS (CYCLOPES) One-eyed giants, sons of Earth and Heaven, employed by Hephaestus in making thunderbolts. In an alternative version, the monsters symbolised by Polyphemus, son of Poseidon, who gravely hindered Odysseus and wooed Galatea.

CYCNUS The name of a number of mythical young men who were changed into a swan.

CYLLARUS The horse of Castor, possibly named after a handsome Centaur killed at the marriage feast of Peirithous.

CYNOSARGES A gymnasium outside Athens reserved for immigrants, where Antisthenes, founder of the Cynics, taught. (Antisthenes seminally influenced Diogenes, the conventional father of the Cynics who was indeed named as a dog because of unconventional 'drop-out' shamelessness.)

CYPRUS Archaelogically known to have sheltered neolithic peoples in the fourth millennium B.C., later colonised successively by Phoenicians, Greeks, Egyptians, Persians and Romans.

CYRENE North African port colonised from Crete c. 630 B.C., later subject to Egypt, later to Rome.

CYRUS 1. The founder of the Persian empire, ruled 559–529 B.C., succeeded by Cambyses. 2. The younger son of Darius II, born c. 425 B.C., who on the accession of his brother Artaxerxes in 405 plotted against him, fought him in 401 but died in battle.

CYTHERA An island off Laconia in the south-east Peloponnesus colonised by Phrygians who made it a centre of the worship of Aphrodite.

D

DACIA The Roman province in the curve of the Danube more recognisable as Transylvania. Previously the Daci had forced the Romans to pay tribute.

DACTYLI Mythical early inhabitants of Mount Ida who worked the iron they mined there.

DAEDALUS Skilled craftsman who left Athens in disgrace after murdering his nephew for jealousy of his technique, went to Crete and made the artificial cow in which Pasiphaë received the bull and conceived the Minotaur, fled with his son Icarus on artificial wings and reached Sicily via Cumae, was pursued by Minos and killed him by pouring molten metal down his bath-taps.

DALMATIA The land on the east of the Adriatic, north of Epirus.

DAMASCUS Capital of the kingdom of Syria, prosperous because of its position on the caravan trail.

DAMOCLES Flattering courtier of Dionysus, tyrant of Syracuse, who was made to assess his happiness by banqueting beneath a sword suspended by a single horse-hair.

DAMON Another courtier of Dionysus of Syracuse who offered to die in the place of his friend Phyntias (not Pythias), condemned for a plot

[83]

against the tyrant. Dionysus reprieved both and sought to be admitted to their bond of friendship.

DANAË Daughter of Acrisius king of Argos, of whom an oracle declared that her son would kill his grandfather. The king shut her up in a tower to prevent intercourse with a male, but Zeus came through in a shower of gold and fathered Perseus.

DANAUS Father of the Danaides, brother of AEGYPTUS, whom see.

DAPHNE Daughter of the river-god Peneus, pursued by Apollo and transformed into a laurel.

DAPHNIS A Sicilian shepherd, son of Hermes, who swore fidelity to the Nymph Echenais, but was seduced in drink by a princess and was blinded by the Nymph. He was taught the flute by Pan and was considered the father of bucolic poetry.

DARDANUS Son of Zeus and Electra and primal ancestor of the Trojans.

DARIUS 1. Darius I, king of Persia 521–486 B.C., whose expedition against the Greeks failed at Marathon, 490. 2. Darius II, king of Persia 424–405 B.C., son of Artaxerxes I.

DECEMVIRI Various colleges of ten Roman magistrates.

DECIUS (CAIUS MESSIUS QUINTUS DECIUS) emperor A.D. 249–251, a vigorous persecutor of the Christians, died in battle against the Goths.

DEIDAMIA Bore a son to Achilles when he was disguised as a girl on the island of Scyrus before the Trojan war.

DELIA The five-yearly festival of Apollo on Delos.

DELOS The birth-place of APOLLO, whom see.

[84]

DAEDALUS AND ICARUS.

DEMETER, OR CERES.

DELPHI The site of the oracle of Apollo on Mount Parnassus.

DEMETER Daughter of Cronus and Rhea, the ancient earth-mother and sister of Zeus who fathered on her Persephone.

DEMETRIUS POLIORCETES Son of Antigonus king of Asia, 336–283 B.C., lost his kingdom of Macedonia and failed to regain Asia, ambitious and capable but licentious and he died of drink in captivity.

DEMOCRITUS Greek philosopher from Thrace, *c.* 460–361 B.C. Noted for his cheerfulness.

DEMOPHOÖN The Son of Celeus whom DEMETER, whom see, failed to make immortal.

DEMOSTHENES 1. Athenian general killed in battle 413 B.C. 2. The supreme Athenian orator, 384–322 B.C., of whose work sixty orations survive.

DEUCALION Son of Prometheus and Clymene, king of Phthia in Thessaly, saved by the gods with his wife Pyrrha when Zeus inundated the world. The ship they built came to rest on Mount Parnassus and they repopulated the land by throwing behind them stones – their interpretation of the gods' command to cast backwards the bones of their mother. The stones sprang up as men and women.

DIAGORAS Lyric poet of Melos known as the Atheist, died *c.* 411 B.C.

DIANA The Etruscan goddess whom the Romans identified with Artemis.

DIOCLETIAN (CAIUS AURELIUS VALERIUS DIOCLETIANUS) Roman emperor A.D. 284–305, divided the empire with Maximianus 286 and subsequently sub-divided it again with Constantius Chlorus and Galerius in 292. Diocletian held the east but abdicated in 305 and retired to Dalmatia, where he had been born in humble status, cultivating his garden for eight years more.

[87]

DIOGENES The name of many philosophers, notably Diogenes the Cynic, *c.* 400–325 B.C., an extremely eccentric man who illustrated his tenets not only in epigrams but in his life – maintaining that nothing natural is indecent and therefore can be done in public: and visibly demonstrating this. He had a celebrated meeting with Alexander the Great.

DIONYSIUS Dionysius I, tyrant of Syracuse *c.* 430–367 B.C., maintained a running war with Carthage and in pursuit of an empire in Sicily and southern Italy.

DIONYSUS After a slow development from a Thracian background emerged as the god of intoxication, handsome but effeminate, worshipped exclusively by women, whose frenzied behaviour during Bacchanalian orgies became notorious.

DIOSCURI The heroes POLYDEUCES and CASTOR, whom see.

DITHYRAMBUS A choral song to Dionysus delivered under the influence of wine.

DODONA A place in the mountains of Epirus where there was an ancient oracle to Zeus.

DOMITIAN (TITUS FLAVIUS DOMITIANUS) born A.D. 51 as younger son of Vespasian (emperor 69–79) and succeeded his brother Titus in 81. His reign was militarily disastrous in the empire and tyrannically vicious at home and he was eventually murdered by his wife Domitia in 96.

DONATUS A 4th century grammarian of Rome who taught Latin to St Jerome and almost every schoolboy since, for his manual became the basis of all Latin grammars.

DORIS 1. A small area in central Greece claimed as their original home by the Dorians who conquered the Peloponnesus. 2. Daughter of Oceanus and Thetis and mother of the 50 Nereids by Nereus who according to some was her brother, according to others the son of Pontus and Mother Earth.

THE DIOSCURI (CASTOR AND POLYDEUCES).

DEUCALION AND PYRRHA.

DRACO (DRACON) Athenian legislator who drew up a code of laws in 621 B.C. with fixed penalties – not discretionary, which favoured the governing class – which were extremely severe, generally death. His code was mitigated by Solon in 594 B.C.

DRUSILLA Second daughter of Germanicus and Agrippina, A.D. 16–38, was first married at the age of 14 and again later but by the time of the accession of her brother Caligula in 37 she was his adored mistress and during the illness in the same year which may have advanced his madness she was named as his heir to the throne – an unprecedented advancement for a woman which was only emphasised when he made her a god after her death in the following year.

DRUSUS I. NERO CLAUDIUS DRUSUS, the son of LIVIA, whom see, born 38 B.C. after her divorce from Tiberius Claudius Nero and her marriage to Octavian (Augustus), and more popular with his stepfather than Livia's elder son Tiberius. Possibly as a consequence he died unexpectedly in 9 B.C. during a successful war in Germany. 2. JULIUS CAESAR DRUSUS, 13 B.C. – A.D. 23, the son of Tiberius and his likely successor as emperor, therefore poisoned by his wife Livilla at the instigation of her lover Sejanus, who aspired to the imperial status.

DRYADS (DRYADES) Nymphs of the trees, associated with the oak.

E

EBURACUM (EBORACUM) Modern York, became the chief Roman settlement in Britain, and the emperors Septimius Severus and Constantius Chlorus died there.

ECHIDNA Half-snake, half-woman who became the mother of the Chimaera, Cerberus and other monsters.

ECHO A Nymph who distracted Hera from Zeus' amorous adventures by constantly talking to her, then fell hopelessly in love with Narcissus and pined away into disembodied sound.

ELAGABALUS Bassianus, called after the Sun-God whom he served as a priest at Emesa in Syria and whose worship with licentious excess he brought to Rome when he became the very youthful emperor Marcus Aurelius Antoninus in A.D. 218. He and his mother Julia Soaemias were murdered in 222.

ELECTRA 1. Daughter of Oceanus, mother of Iris and the Harpies. 2. Daughter of Agamemnon and Clytaemnestra who preserved her young brother Orestes after the murder of their father and was later his accomplice in the killing of their mother.

ELEUSIS Town in Attica inferior only to Athens, the site of the temple to Demeter and the Eleusinian mysteries honouring Demeter and Persephone.

DIANA OF EPHESUS.

EOS, OR AURORA.

ELIS The plain in the north-west Peloponnesus south of Arcadia.

ELYSIUM Originally a happy land in the Ocean to which favoured heroes pass without dying, later an area in the lower world reserved for the élite.

ENDYMION A beautiful young king of Elis beloved by Selene and moon-charmed into perpetual sleep so that she might perpetually kiss him.

EOS The dawn-goddess, daughter of Hyperion and Thea, married to Tithonus but consistently faithless to him, which accounts for the blush of dawn.

EPHESUS Became the principal Ionian city on the coast of Asia Minor at the mouth of the Cayster.

EPHORS Dorian magistrates, notably the five co-sovereigns of Sparta.

EPICTETUS Stoic philosopher of Hierapolis in Phrygia, c. A.D. 55–135, expelled from Rome in 89 and thenceforth taught at Nicopolis in Epirus.

EPICURUS Philosopher 342–270 B.C., born in Samos, established his school in Athens 306 and admitted women to his garden-academy, taught that the outcome of virtue was supreme happiness.

EPIDAURUS A town in Argos preserving a 4th century B.C. theatre, the centre of the cult of Asclepius (Aesculapius).

EPIRUS Literally the mainland of Greece.

EREBOS (EREBUS) God of darkness, son of Chaos the sister of Night.

ERETRIA A maritime and commercial city of Euboea.

ERINNA 4th century B.C. Lesbian poet of the island of Telos who died at the age of 19 and was critically admired.

ERIS The goddess of discord who prompted the quarrel in Olympia which led to the judgement of Paris and the Trojan war.

EROS The wanton boy-god of physical desire, son of Aphrodite by Ares or Hermes or Zeus.

ETRUSCANS Highly cultivated early people of central Italy who passed much of their religion on to the Romans and were famous for divining.

EUBOEA The long island opposite Attica, Boeotia and Thessaly, a centre of strategic intrigue.

EUCLID (EUCLIDES) Mathematician of Alexandria, *fl.* 300 B.C.

EUMENIDES (ERINYES) The avenging spirits of punishment, Tisiphone, Alecto and Megaera.

EUPHROSYNE One of the Graces.

EURIPIDES Tragic playwright, 480–406 B.C., born in Salamis, won dramatic contests in Athens from 441 for 20 of his 92 plays, intellectually a modernist sceptical of contemporary religion.

EURYDICE The wife of ORPHEUS, whom see.

EUTERPE The Muse of the flutes.

EROS OF PRAXITELES.

THE FATES, OR THE MOIRAI.

F

FABIUS (QUINTUS FABIUS MAXIMUS CUNCTATOR)
Five times consul in Rome, 233–209 B.C., dictator 217 when he imposed the delaying 'scorched earth' policy against Hannibal but could not muster the final blow, died 203.

FALERNUS AGER A wine-growing district in Campania.

FASCES Symbol of Etruscan, later Roman, authority, a bundle of wooden rods enclosing an axe borne as a mace by lictors before magistrates.

FATES The Moirai who apply the decrees of individual destiny: Lachesis who chooses the individual, Clotho who spins the thread of events, Atropos who executes it. To the Romans they were Parcae.

FLAMINIUS (TITUS QUINCTIUS FLAMINIUS)
Roman general and statesman, consul 198 B.C. before his 30th birthday, used high diplomacy to contain autonomous Greece.

FLAMINIUS (CAIUS FLAMINIUS)
Popular reformist tribune of the plebs in Rome 232 B.C., successful general 223, censor 220 when he built the Circus Flaminius and the great northern highway Via Flaminia.

FLORA The Roman goddess of flowers and Spring.

FORNAX The Roman goddess of baking in the oven.

FORTUNA The Roman goddess of good luck, Tyche to the Greeks.

FORTUNATORUM INSULAE The Isles of the Blessed, the early conception of the fields of Elysium.

FORUM An open space of ground for public use. Later in Rome the magnificent FORUM ROMANUM between the Capitoline and the Palatine Hills.

FRONTINUS (SEXTUS JULIUS FRONTINUS) A.D 30–104, Governor of Britain 74–78, Roman author of technical works on military science and civil engineering.

FULVIA The politically active wife, in succession, of Clodius, Curio and Mark Antony, died 40 B.C.

ONE OF THE EUMENIDES, OR ERINYES.

GANYMEDE.

G

GABII An extinct city near Rome where traditionally Romulus was brought up.

GADES Modern Cadiz, founded from Tyre *c.* 1100 B.C., a base for Hamilcar Barca, an ally of Rome from 206 B.C.

GALATEA A Nymph of the sea beloved by POLYPHEMUS and ACIS, whom see.

GALATIA Originally a part of central Asia Minor embracing areas of Phrygia and Cappadocia, named after the Gauls, later a Roman province, from 25 B.C., its boundaries varying through the years.

GALEN (CLAUDIUS GALENUS) Physician born at Pergamum A.D. 130, practised in Rome 162–166 and 169 until his death in 200, a pioneer in anatomy and psychological medicine.

GALLIA The Gauls, or Celts, controlled in their time land from Galicia to Galatia, but in historical nomenclature Gallia Transalpina comprised modern France with its natural boundaries of water and mountains (Caesar's 'three parts' were Aquitania, Celtica and Belgica) and Gallia Cisalpina covered modern northern Italy.

GALLIENUS· (PUBLIUS LICINIUS EGNATIUS GALLIENUS) was an ineffectual Roman emperor A.D. 260–268.

GALLUS (CAIUS VIBIUS TREBONIANUS GALLUS) was a disastrous Roman emperor A.D. 251–253.

GANYMEDE A pretty boy mortal carried off by Zeus to be a cup-bearer to the gods.

GAZA A Philistine city captured by Alexander the Great.

GE (GAEA)Mother-Earth, called Tellus by the Romans, sprang from Chaos and bore her son Uranus while she slept. By Uranus she gave birth to the Titans, and encouraged one of them, Cronus, to emasculate his father (see APHRODITE).

GELA A city in Sicily where Gelon became tyrant, afterwards reigning at Syracuse and defeating the Carthaginians, and where Aeschylus died.

GEMONIAE A flight of steps in Rome down which the strangled bodies of executed prisoners were dragged and flung into the river.

GERMANIA A country roughly 'co-terminous with the Greater Reich of Hitler which was never conquered by the Romans.

GERMANICUS JULIUS CAESAR Born 15 B.C. and adopted by his uncle Tiberius, whom he served as a military aide in Germany and later, when Tiberius was emperor, as a successful general there. Tiberius jealously recalled him in A.D. 17 and sent him to Syria, where he died in 19, it is believed poisoned by the governor, Piso.

GERYON (GERYONES) A three-headed king of Spain whose choice oxen were driven away by Heracles.

GIGANTES The giants who sprang from the blood cast on the earth by the maiming of Uranus who later attacked the gods with rocks flung to heaven, and after defeat were suitably buried in volcanoes.

GLAUCUS Commander of the Lycians before Troy who recognised his old comrade Diomedes in the fray and refused to fight him but ex-changed armour with him.

GE, OR GAEA.

GORDIAN (MARCUS ANTONIUS GORDIANUS) The name of three successive emperors of Rome A.D. 238–244.

GORDIUS King of Phrygia and father of Midas who, on accession dedicated his chariot to Zeus, fastening the pole to the yoke with a knot of bark which the oracle foretold would be untied only by the man who would rule both Europe and Asia. Alexander the Great cut it with his sword.

GORGONES (GORGONS) Winged, serpent-haired and sharp-clawed female monsters, Stheno, Euryale and Medusa, of whom Medusa alone was mortal and by far the ugliest, the sight of her head turning the beholder to stone. Perseus cut it off, using a mirror for an accurate stroke, and Athena placed it on her shield, or her breastplate.

GOTHS The Gothi or Guttones, originating in Gotland, were a Germanic people particularly active from the 3rd century A.D. menacing the eastern and western empires.

GRACCHUS The name of members of a Roman family, notably of 'the Gracchi', TIBERIUS SEMPRONIUS GRACCHUS and his younger brother CAIUS SEMPRONIUS GRACCHUS, who lost their father in early life and were diligently educated by CORNELIA, whom see. Tiberius, tribune in 133 B.C., proposed agrarian reform which would re-create a property-owning peasantry. It was vigorously opposed by the aristocracy, and Tiberius was assassinated in 132 by his cousin Scipio Nasica. Caius Gracchus took over the organisation of the newly-founded Popular party and, as tribune of the plebs in 123 B.C. and again in 122, proposed radical reforms giving the lower class more constitutional power as well as passing the new agrarian law. Meeting violent opposition later, he committed suicide through the sword of his slave in 121 and some thousands of his supporters were killed.

GRAEAE Three old women possessing one eye and one tooth between them, which they passed round at need, said to be sisters of the Gorgons.

GRAECIA Territory occupied by the Graeci or Hellenes, and thus comprising not only modern Greece but also MAGNA GRAECIA, the area in southern Italy where Greek cities were founded.

GRATIANUS Emperor of the west A.D. 367–383.

GRYPHUS A griffin, having the body of a lion and the head and wings of an eagle said to guard stores of gold.

GYAS (GYES, GYGES) A giant with 100 hands, son of Uranus and Ge.

GYGES First king of Lydia, *c.* 685–657 B.C.

HADES THRONED.

H

HADES (AIDES) The son of Cronus and Rhea, brother of Zeus, and lord of the lower world, tactfully called by the Romans PLUTO as the provider of wealth from mined minerals. He was grim and inexorable, but not essentially evil. His queen was Persephone. He carried a staff with which he beckoned the dying to the lower world.

HADRIAN (PUBLIUS AELIUS HADRIANUS) Born in Rome A.D. 76, gained the favour of Trajan and was groomed as emperor, ruling A.D. 117–138. He toured the empire dutifully but spent significant time in Greece, which he greatly favoured. Apart from provoking the desperate Jewish revolt of 132–135, he consolidated peace, culture and efficient administration.

HALICARNASSUS A city of Caria in Asia Minor noted for the Mausoleum, (see ARTEMISIA).

HAMILCAR BARCA Carthaginian general active in the latter part of the first Punic war and later conqueror of Spain, died 229 B.C.

HANNIBAL Eldest son of Hamilcar Barca, born 247 B.C., on the death of Hasdrubal (1) continued the Carthaginian conquest of Spain until 219, mounted his attack on Italy 218, won the great victory of Cannae 216, unsuccessfully marched against Rome 211, withdrew to Africa 203 and conceded final defeat to Scipio Africanus at Zama, 202. Was later engaged in war from Syria and committed suicide in 183 to avoid extradition to the Romans.

HARMONIA Daughter of Ares and Aphrodite, given as wife to Cadmus of Thebes by Zeus with the wedding present of a necklace which proved fatal to all who wore it.

HARPALUS Macedonian treasurer to Alexander the Great who embezzled the treasury at Babylon in 324 B.C., crossed to Greece and bribed Athenian statesmen including Demosthenes to support him. Killed 323.

HARPIES (HARPYIAE) Three flying spirits, Aello, Ocypete and Celaeno, expert abductors and torturers.

HASDRUBAL 1. Son-in-law of Hamilcar Barca, took over the Carthaginian command in Spain 229 B.C., founded New Carthage and drew up a treaty partitioning Spain with the Romans. Assassinated 221. 2. Younger son of Hamilcar Barca and brother of Hannibal, fought the Romans in Spain 218–207 B.C., when he marched into Italy and was killed in the defeat on the Metaurus, 207 B.C.

HEBE (JUVENTAS to the Romans) The daughter of Zeus and Hera, goddess of youth and cup-bearer to the gods before Ganymede was conscripted. She became the wife of Ares and had some powers of bestowing eternal youth.

HECATE An ancient goddess of the earth, later associated with the moon, became the confidant of Persephone in the land of Hades and a powerful mistress of sorcery and night phantoms: a primeval witch.

HECTOR Trojan hero, the eldest son of Priam and Hecuba, husband of Andromache and father of Astyanax. Finally killed by Achilles and his body desecrated before its ransom by Priam.

HECUBA (HECUBE) Principal wife of Priam of Troy, and mother of 18 of his 50 sons including Hector. She was carried away as a slave, after many vicissitudes she blinded the Thracian Polymestor who had killed her son Polydorus, and the curse was uttered against her that she would turn to a bitch before her death.

HELEN (HELENE, HELENA) The daughter of Zeus and Leda and

HARPIES, OR HARPYIAE.

HELIOS, OR SOL.

sister of the Dioscuri, was seized in her youth by Theseus of Athens but rescured by the Dioscuri. She returned to Sparta, eventually married Menelaus, but was seduced by Paris with the help of Aphrodite and they eloped to Troy.

HELENA (FLAVIA JULIA HELENA) The Christian mother of Constantine the Great who discovered in Jerusalem the Holy Sepulchre and the true Cross.

HELENUS Son of Priam and Hecuba possessing the gift of prophecy, came into the hands of the Greeks at Troy, eventually married Andromache.

HELICON Mountain range in Boeotia sacred to Apollo and the Muses. Site of the spring Hippocrene, struck by the hoof of Pegasus from the rock.

HELIOS The god of the Sun, SOL to the Romans, son of Hyperion and Thea and brother of Selene and Eos, drove a four-horse chariot (once commandeered by Phaethon) daily across the sky and at night was ferried eastwards by Oceanus.

HELLEN Son of Deucalion and Pyrrha, king of Phthia in Thessaly, founder of the Hellene race.

HELLESPONT The 50-mile strait connecting the Aegean with the sea of Marmora, bridged by Xerxes near Sestos and Abydos across which Leander swam to Hero; named after Helle, who was riding over the strait on an airborne ram with a golden fleece when she toppled and fell into the sea.

HELVETII Celts of modern western Switzerland, in conflict with the Romans 107–58 B.C.

HEPHAESTUS (VULCAN to the Romans) The smith-god of fire, son of Zeus and Hera, either born lame or lamed by being thrown from Olympus by Zeus when he championed his mother in a quarrel with his father, and consequently became a craftsman constructing many magical

[113]

toys and novelties for the gods. He married Aphrodite, and during one of her infidelities, caught her and Ares in bed in a fine metal net and exposed them to the ridicule of the gods.

HERA (HERE, assimilated by the Romans with JUNO) The daughter of Cronus and Rhea, sister of Zeus whose wife she later became, and by him the mother of Ares, Hebe and Hephaestus. The goddess of marriage and a divinity of childbirth, she was nevertheless given qualities of shrewishness and jealousy against all the mortal children of Zeus, and bore a particular animosity against Troy.

HERACLEA The name of a number of cities dedicated to Heracles.

HERACLES (HERCULES) A great Greek hero, conceived by ALCMENE, whom see, as the result of a shady ploy by Zeus. Hera sent snakes to kill him in his cradle, but the infant strangled them. As he grew up he performed great feats of strength and valour, but after he was married to Megara Hera sent him mad, and he killed his children. For purification he was bound in service to Eurystheus, who assigned to him the famous twelve labours, apparently impossible, which he had to perform. Later he accomplished many other wonderful deeds.

HERACLITUS A philosopher of Ephesus, *fl. c.* 500 B.C.

HERCULANEUM A former Grecian colony near Naples damaged by an eruption of Vesuvius in A.D. 63 and totally destroyed in 79.

HERMS (HERMAE) Marble or bronze pillars originally erected to Hermes but later carved with the heads of other gods, often with male genitals added in the block below the bust. They were common in the streets of Athens in the 5th century B.C., and were the occasion for vandalism and graffiti. Alcibiades was banished for defacing one in 415 B.C.

HERMAPHRODITUS The son of Hermes and Aphrodite, said to have been embraced by an infatuated Nymph with the prayer to the gods that their bodies should be united for ever. Statues bearing women's breasts and male genitals were carved from the 4th century B.C.

HERA, or JUNO.

HERMES, OR MERCURY.

HERMES (identified by the Romans as MERCURIUS, MERCURY) The son of Zeus and Maia, he demonstrated mischiefs and cunning from the day of his birth, stealing Apollo's cattle, inventing the lyre, trading godlike qualities with Apollo and cozening from Zeus a place on Olympus. He became the herald of the gods and the escort of the shades of the dead. He was the god of travellers, the patron of music and of gymnastics and of many other skills. He wore a characteristic travelling hat, the petasus, and a ribboned or serpent-twined wand, the caduceus.

HERO Priestess of Aphrodite at Sestos, used to place a light to guide her lover Leander as he swam the Hellespont at night from Abydos to visit her. When a storm extinguished the light Leander was drowned.

HERODES 1. Herod the Great, king of Judaea from 43 B.C. by the gift of Mark Antony, confirmed by Octavian in 30. Ruthless in government and in his domestic life, he died 4 B.C. 2. Herod Antipas, took the tetrarchies of Galilee and Peraea (but not the kingdom of Judaea) on the death of his father, Herod the Great. Deposed by Caligula in A.D. 39.

HERODOTUS Greek historian, born at Halicarnassus in 484 B.C., joined the Greek colony at Thurii in Lucania, southern Italy about 443 after extensive travelling, and he probably continued intermittent travelling before beginning what was virtually a history of the known world until 478 B.C. He died in 425.

HESIOD (HESIODUS) Greek didactic poet of the 8th century B.C.

HESPERIDES The daughters of Atlas and Hesperis (the female variant of Hesperus, the evening star) who guarded the golden apples given by Ge to Hera at her marriage to Zeus. Heracles had to recover the apples.

HESPERUS The evening star, son of Eos, possibly by Atlas.

HESTIA (VESTA to the Romans) The goddess of the hearth, daughter of Cronus and Rhea, a devoted virgin although goddess of domestic life.

HIBERNIA Ireland, first known to and named by the Greeks 525 B.C.

HIERON Ruler of Gela in Sicily and later tyrant of Syracuse 478–467 B.C., made his court a haven of culture and gave hospitality to Aeschylus, Pindar and many philosophers and poets.

HIERONYMUS 1. Early companion in arms of Alexander the Great, wrote an important work of history, died *c.* 250 B.C. 2. Eusebius Hieronymus, *c.* A.D. 348–420, born in Dalmatia and educated in Rome, became a Christian priest about 381, re-translated the Bible into Latin (the Vulgate), settled in Bethlehem about 386 and died 420. Canonised as Saint Jerome.

HIPPO The north African see of St. Augustine as bishop.

HIPPOCRATES 5th century B.C. physician born in Cos whose reputation has come down as the ideal doctor and whose teaching traditionally fathered scientific medicine, although none of his original works remain.

HIPPOCRENE The fountain on HELICON, which see, haunt of the Muses and the inspiration of poets.

HIPPOLYTE Queen of the Amazons whose girdle Heracles secured.

HIPPOLYTUS Son of Theseus and Hippolyte, wooed by his step-mother Phaedra, cursed by his father and killed through the agency of Poseidon. Artemis persuaded Asclepius to resuscitate him.

HISPANIA The Roman name for modern Spain. The Greeks called it Iberia.

HOMER The epic poet who wrote the *Iliad* and the *Odyssey*, or at least the original master who compiled the drafts of the poems known today, possibly using more ancient verses as symphonic composers commandeer folk-tunes. Born either at Chios or at Smyrna (though five other cities confidently claimed him), traditionally a blind bard, writing before 700 B.C.: that is the meagre best that can be said with certainty about the composer of what are artistically the most influential literary works in the world.

THE GIRDLE OF HIPPOLYTE.

HONORIUS FLAVUS Roman emperor of the west A.D. 395–423, during which time Alaric the Visigoth sacked Rome.

HOPLITES Heavily armed Greek infantry fighting in phalanx formation.

HORAE The goddesses of the seasons, first three then four, daughters of Zeus and Themis, the protagonist of good order.

HORATIUS COCLES Horace One-Eyed, a fabulous Roman who held back the Etruscans from the wooden Sublician bridge while the engineers demolished it, and although severely wounded swam back across the Tiber.

HORATIUS FLACCUS (HORACE) Roman lyric poet, born in Apulia 65 B.C., educated in Rome and Athens, where he joined the army of Brutus in 44 and fled at Philippi. Chastened in Rome he became friendly with Maecenas in 38 and accepted from him in 33 the Sabine farm which comfortably supported him, scintillating in the Augustan scene and friendly even with Augustus.

HORTENSIUS (QUINTUS HORTENSIUS) Roman orator, advocate and administrator 114–50 B.C.

HORUS (HARPOCRATES) Egyptian god, the son of Isis, worshipped in Greece.

HUNS (HUNNI) Asiatics who came to Thrace in the 4th century A.D. and in the next century devastated Europe.

HYACINTHUS Exquisite youth loved by Apollo and Zephyrus and preferring Apollo, killed by a quoit loosed by Apollo but diverted by Zephyrus, and the hyacinth flower sprang from his blood.

HYADES The Rainers, a group of five or seven stars in the constellation of Taurus, originally nymphs who wept until they died after their brother Hyas died.

HYGEIA Goddess of health, daughter of Asclepius.

HYMEN (HYMENAEUS) The god of marriage, his name invented from a salutation in the Greek wedding ceremony.

HYMETTUS A mountain near Athens renowned for marble and honey.

HYPERION Titan son of Uranus and Ge, father of Helios, Selene and Eos.

HYPERMNESTRA The single daughter of Danaus who spared her husband in the slaughter by the Danaids. See AEGYPTUS.

HYPNUS (HYPNOS) The Greek god of sleep.

THE SACRIFICE OF IPHIGENIA.

I

IACCHUS A god, invented like Hymen from a ceremonial cry in the Eleusinian mysteries of Dionysus, later identified with Bacchus.

IAPETUS Titan son of Uranus and Ge, father of Atlas and Prometheus and Epimetheus by Clymene.

IASION Son of Zeus and Electra, father of Pluto by Demeter.

IBERIA The Greek names for 1. Spain, 2. an area south of the Caucasus, modern Georgia.

ICARUS The son of Daedalus who failed to complete his flight from Crete.

ICENI The British tribe based on Venta Icenorum (modern Caister) who revolted under their queen Boudicca.

ICTINUS The Greek architect who collaborated in the building of the Parthenon, late 5th century B.C.

IDA Mountain range in Asia Minor, scene of the judgement of Paris, and the vantage point from which the gods observed the battle for Troy.

IDOMENEUS King of Crete, grandson of Minos, led the Cretans to Troy vowed to Poseidon during a storm on his return to sacrifice the first creature he met on landing, and was confronted by his own son.

IDUS (IDES) The 13th or the 15th day of the month in Rome.

ILITHYIA The Greek goddess who aided women in childbirth.

ILUS Son of Tros and grandfather of Priam, the founder of Ilion (Troy).

INDIA Used by the Greeks and Romans to signify south-east Asia.

INFAMIA The Roman penalty of loss of civil rights.

INFERI The gods of the lower world, sometimes all the dead.

IO The daughter of Inachus king of Argos, changed by Zeus into a heifer to conceal his passion for her, identified by Hera and placed under the surveillance of the hundred-eyed Argus, who was killed by Hermes, but Io was driven by a gadfly from pasture to pasture and across the Bosporus until she recovered her original form on the banks of the Nile and bore her son Epaphus.

IOLCUS City in Thessaly from which Jason sailed to seek the golden fleece.

IONIA The coastal strip of Asia Minor settled by the Ionian Greeks.

IOPHON Dramatist son of Sophocles, said to have tried to acquire his father's property by alleging his senility.

IPHIGENIA Daughter of AGAMEMNON and Clytaemnestra who would have been sacrificed by her father, whom see, had not Artemis intervened and carried her off to be a priestess in Tauris. She later saved her brother Orestes when he, too, would have been sacrificed to Artemis.

IRENE (PAX to the Romans). The goddess of peace.

IRIS A messenger of the gods, the personification of the rainbow.

ISIS The Egyptian goddess, wife of Osiris and mother of Horus, sporadic-

IRIS.

HEBE, OR JUVENTAS.

ally recognised by the Greeks as Demeter but much more significantly worshipped by the Romans who identified her with Ceres.

ISOCRATES An Athenian orator, 436–338 B.C.

ITALIA Originally southern Italy, the land occupied by the Siculi, also known as Itali; later, all the country south of the Alps, that is, modern Italy.

ITHACA An island in the Ionian sea off Epirus, the birthplace of Odysseus.

ITIUS PORTUS The harbour from which Caesar sailed to invade Britain, probably modern Wissant, near Calais.

IXION King of the Lapiths, renowned in Greek myth for the first man to murder a kinsman, who killed his father-in-law to avoid paying the bride-price at his wedding. Zeus took him to Olympus to purify him but he tried to seduce Hera. Zeus presented him with a cloud resembling Hera on which he begot the first Centaur. As punishment, Hermes chained him by hands and feet to a wheel which constantly revolves in the sky.

J

JANUS An Italic deity signifying 'the beginning', represented either by a gate or by a two-headed statue (because every gate opens two ways). His temple in the Roman Forum had its two doors shut in time of peace, which occurred only on three occasions in Roman history.

JASON Son of Aeson king of Iolcus, in infancy escaped murder by his usurping uncle Pelias and was brought up by Chiron. In maturity he demanded his kingdom from Pelias, who first set him the task of annexing the golden fleece of king Acëtes of Colchis, which was guarded by a dragon. He set sail in the ship Argo with the Argonauts, the fabulous heroes of Greece. After many adventures he was successful, with the magical help of MEDEA, whom see.

JERUSALEM (HIEROSOLYMA) First verified as a city by literary reference c. 1400 B.C. when garrisoned by the Egyptians, was captured by David about 1050 B.C., was destroyed by Nebuchadnezzar of Babylon 558 B.C., was rebuilt c. 538–516 B.C., captured by the Roman Pompey in 63, razed by Titus in A.D. 70, rebuilt by Hadrian in A.D. 135.

JOCASTA The mother of Oedipus, whom she innocently married, and the mother by him of Antigone and others.

JOSEPHUS (FLAVIUS JOSEPHUS) Jewish general and historian A.D. 38–c. 100, governor of Galilee in 67, defeated by the Romans and witnessed as a prisoner the sacking of Jerusalem.

JANUS.

JUPITER.

JUBA 1. King of Numidia who joined Pompey against Julius Caesar, died after defeat in battle 46 B.C. 2. Son of preceding, educated in Rome, made king of Numidia by Octavian in 30 B.C. and married to Cleopatra the daughter of Antony and Cleopatra. Died as King of Mauretania A.D. 19.

JUGURTHA Joint king of Numidia from 118 B.C., sole king after the necessary assassinations from 112, skilfully manipulated the Romans who moved against him but was finally overcome by Marius, graced his triumph in Rome, and was strangled in prison 104 B.C.

JULIA 1. Daughter of Julius Caesar and Cornelia, married Pompey in 59 B.C., died in childbirth 54. 2. The only child of Augustus, born 39 B.C., first married at the age of 14 to her cousin Marcellus who died two years later, then to Agrippa who died 12 B.C., then to Tiberius, but in 2 B.C. her father banished her for immorality and she died at Rhegium (modern Reggio Calabria) in A.D. 14 soon after her husband's accession. 3. Daughter of the preceding and Agrippa, 19 B.C.–A.D. 28, also banished by Augustus for immorality.

JULIANUS (FLAVIUS CLAUDIUS JULIANUS) The emperor Julian the Apostate, ruled A.D. 361–363, born 331, the nephew of Constantine the Great, escaped the massacre of Constantine's kinsmen in 337, was a successful general in Gaul when he succeeded emperor Constantius 361 and declared himself a pagan. Many of the writings of this enlightened man survive. He died while campaigning against the Persians.

JUNO Ancient Italian goddess concerned with all aspects of the life of women, gradually assimilated to Hera and made queen of heaven to Jupiter, but without the attribution of Hera's more human, womanly abandonment of godlike dignity.

JUPITER Primitive Italian sky-god who later inherited some of the more mischievous history attributed to Zeus, but mainly occupied a status that was more aweful, combining the omnipotence of Jehovah with the sanctity of Roman virtue and the majesty of Roman power with which he became materially associated.

JUSTINIAN (FLAVIUS PETRUS SABBATIUS IUSTIN-
IANUS) Roman emperor of the east A.D. 527–565, born 482 the
nephew of the emperor Justinus, on succession conducted vigorous war
against the Persians and re-conquered the west, was involved in theological controversy, re-codified the laws which established the lasting
framework of Roman law in Europe.

JUVENAL (DECIMUS IUNIUS IUVENALIS) Roman satiric
poet *c.* A.D. 60–140. No details of his life survive, but 16 forceful and
informative satires remain.

L

LACEDAEMON The popular name for Sparta.

LAELAPS The name of the swift, unerring hound given to CEPHALUS, whom see, and the name of the storm wind.

LAERTES King of Ithaca, an Argonaut and a participator in the hunt for the Calydonian boar, the father of Odysseus who welcomed him back from Troy.

LAIS The name of two separate but renowned Greek courtesans operating in Corinth.

LAIUS King of Thebes, father of Oedipus by JOCASTA, whom see, accidentally killed by OEDIPUS, whom see.

LALAGE A characteristic nickname for a Greek courtesan, literally Chatterbox.

LAMIA 1. The name of a bogey-woman used to frighten children. 2. The chief city of Malis in Thessaly, seized by Antipater of Macedonia who was besieged by the Greeks there in the Lamian war of 323–322 B.C.

LANGOBARDI (LONGOBARDI) The Lombards, a German tribe which settled in north Italy in the 6th century A.D.

LAOCOON Trojan prince, the brother of Anchises, who tried to dissuade the Trojans from drawing the wooden horse into the city. In his capacity as priest of Apollo, some say of Poseidon, Laocoon and his two sons were attacked by two great snakes after having offended the god. The famous sculpture of this event, now in the Vatican, dates from the 1st century B.C. and was worked in Rhodes by Agesander, Polydorus and Athenodorus.

LAOMEDON King of Troy, father of Priam, offended Poseidon and Apollo who had been sentenced by Zeus for a misdemeanour to work for him – Poseidon built the walls of Troy. Poseidon sent a sea-dragon to ravage the country. Heracles killed it when Laomedon's daughter Hesione was to be sacrificed to it. Laomedon cheated Heracles of his reward, so the hero sailed into Troy and killed Laomedon and all his family except Priam. He gave Hesione to Telamon.

LAPITHS (LAPITHAE) A people in Thessaly ruled by Pirithous, a son of Ixion and therefore half-brother to the Centaurs. In the bloody quarrel at the wedding feast of Pirithous the Centaurs failed to carry off his bride Hippodamia and a company of other ladies.

LARES To the Romans, spirits of dead ancestors which watched benignly over a household.

LARVAE Malign spirits of the dead.

LATINUS King of Latium who gave his daughter Lavinia to be married to Aeneas.

LATIUM The country in Italy between Etruria and Campania.

LATMUS The mountain in Caria where Selene woos Endymion.

LAVERNA Roman goddess protecting thieves and frauds.

LEANDER The youth of Abydos who swam to HERO, whom see.

LEDA Wife of Tyndareus king of Sparta, ravished by Zeus as a swan,

HECATE.

HEPHAESTUS, OR VULCAN.

and giving birth to Helen and Polydeuces from one egg. But CASTOR, whom see, was conceived as the son of Tyndareus on the same night, and born on the same day as his 'twin' Polydeuces (Pollux).

LEMANUS LACUS Modern Lake Geneva (Lac du Leman).

LEMURES The ghosts of the dead, both LARES and LARVAE, whom see.

LEONIDAS 1. King of Sparta, ruled 487–480 B.C., held the pass at Thermopylae against the Persians successfully for two days until all but he and his 300 Spartans fled. They remained to cover the retreat of the fleet from Artemisium and died. 2. 3rd century B.C. Greek epigrammatist well represented in the Anthology, concerned himself with the conditions of the poor.

LEONNATUS A Macedonian general of Alexander the Great who after the king's death was defeated by the Athenians 322 B.C.

LEOTYCHIDES King of Sparta, ruled c. 491–469 B.C., heavily beat the Persians in a land and sea battle 479.

LEPIDUS 1. MARCUS AEMILIUS LEPIDUS, consul in Rome 78 B.C., tried to revive the Popular party, marched on Rome, but retreated to Sardinia and died. 2. MARCUS AEMILIUS LEPIDUS, son of the preceding, praetor in 49 B.C., consul with Caesar 46, on the assassination in 44 supported Mark Antony with an army, took Caesar's position as pontifex maximus, went to Gaul, was joined by a defeated Antony, marched back and they were joined by Octavian, they formed the triumvirate and Lepidus took Spain as well as Gaul. Triumvir 42–36 when, after intrigues, he was forced into private life (remaining pontifex maximus) and died in 13 B.C.

LERNA Marshy river near Argos where Heracles killed the Lernean Hydra.

LESBOS Island off Asia Minor which became the cradle of Aeoliad lyric poetry and the literal birthplace of the poets Terpander, Alcaeus and Sappho and many other intellectual lions.

LETHE The river in the lower world from which the shades drank and thus obtained forgetfulness of living.

LETO (LATONA to the Romans) Titaness daughter of Coeus and Phoebe and mother by Zeus of APOLLO and ARTEMIS (whom see) on Delos and Ortygia.

LIBANIUS Greek philosopher *c.* A.D. 314–395, tutor to the Saints Basil and Chrysostom and intimate of the apostate emperor Julian, has a number of works extant and has been called the last of the Hellenists.

LIBERTAS A contrived Roman goddess of political freedom and constitutional government, significantly given a temple by TIBERIUS SEMPRONIUS GRACCHUS (whom see) in 238 B.C. and later appearing in statues as wearing the Phrygian cap of liberty.

LIBITINA An ancient Italian goddess, originally associated with voluptuous or libidinous pleasures but later identified, possibly in the place of Persephone, as the goddess of death, burial, and undertakers.

LIBYA The Greek name for Africa, not merely the northern part.

LICINIUS (VALERIUS LICINIANUS) Formally a Roman emperor A.D. 308–323, was raised to the rank of Augustus by emperor Galerius in 308 and when Galerius died in 310 he allied himself with Constantine and allowed him to destroy one rival Augustus, Maxentius, while he himself destroyed another, Maximinus. Later he quarrelled with Constantine, who defeated and deposed him in 323. He died in 324.

LIGURIA The coastal strip from modern Genoa to Monaco.

LILYBAEUM Town in Sicily founded from Carthage in 396 B.C. as the nearest point to Africa and extensively used as a military channel-port. Modern Marsala.

LINDUM COLONIA Roman colony on the road from London to York, modern Lincoln.

LINUS Originally the name of a wailing lamentation, later personified as Linus, a son of Apollo born to a princess Psamathe, who exposed the child in shame. He was brought up by shepherds but was later torn to pieces by dogs. At propitiation sacrifices to Linus and Psamathe the wailing was exercised.

LIVIA DRUSILLA The beautiful and cultured *éminence grise* behind the emperor Augustus whom she married at the age of 20 in 38 B.C. after Augustus had forcibly divorced her from Tiberius Claudius Nero: she had borne her first husband a son, Tiberius, later emperor, and was pregnant with DRUSUS, whom see, who became a favourite of Augustus until he died. Livia had no children by Augustus. Her part in the extraordinary succession of deaths which virtually forced Augustus to name Tiberius as his successor is a matter of controversy. When Tiberius came to power in A.D. 14 he gradually excluded his mother from influence and she died in advanced old age in A.D. 29.

LIVILLA Daughter-in-law of Tiberius: see DRUSUS (2).

LIVIUS ANDRONICUS (LUCIUS LIVIUS ANDRONI-CUS) A Greek, *c.* 284–204 B.C., brought to Rome as a slave and freed by his master Lucius Livius, graduated from literature to posts in the theatre and became the first original playwright in Latin.

LIVY (TITUS LIVIUS) Roman historian, 59 B.C.–A.D. 17, was born and died in Padua but spent his working life in Rome, and wrote the complete history of the state over eight centuries in 142 books, a task which took him forty years. Only 35 books remain.

LOCRI EPIZEPHYRII An ancient city in southern Italy near Brindisi colonised by the Greeks in 700 B.C.

LOCUSTA (LUCUSTA) An expert woman poisoner employed, among other commissions, by Agrippina to murder Claudius and by her son Nero to murder Claudius' son Britannicus.

LONDINIUM (LONDINUM) Modern London, sacked during the revolt of Boudicca, gradually became the logistic, financial, and possibly the administrative capital of Roman Britain and received the title Augusta in the mid-4th century A.D.

LONGINUS (CASSIUS LONGINUS) A Greek philosopher, *c.* A.D. 213–273 who practised in Athens.

LUCANIA An area in southern Italy south of Campania.

LUCANUS (MARCUS ANNAEUS LUCANUS, LUCAN) Roman poet, born in Corduba (Cordova), Spain in A.D. 39, educated in Rome, committed forcible suicide after the discovery of a plot against Nero, 65.

LUCIAN Greek sophist, rhetorician and brilliant essayist born in Syria A.D. 120.

LUCIFER (PHOSPHORUS) The bringer of light, as applied to the the planet Venus, personified in mythology as a male, though the name is used as a suffix for Artemis and Aurora.

LUCILIUS (CAIUS LUCILIUS) Roman satirist and friend of Scipio, 180–102 B.C.

LUCINA Juno in the role of the goddess who brings children to the light through birth.

LUCRETIA The wife of Tarquinius Collatinus whose rape by Sextus Tarquinius led to the rising by Junius Brutus and the end of kingship among the Romans by the expulsion of Tarquinius Superbus, father of Sextus.

LUCRETIUS (TITUS LUCRETIUS CARUS) Skilful didactic poet of philosophy, 94–55 B.C., renowned for the *De rerum naturae.*

LUCULLUS (LUCIUS LICINIUS) Roman imperialist general who pacified Asia 74–66 B.C. and at the age of 50 retired to Rome, cold-shouldered, and cultivated a life of elegant indolence.

LUNA The Roman goddess of the moon, comparable to Selene.

LUPERCALIA Roman festival held in the Lupercal, a cave beneath the Palatine hill, on 15 February annually, a lusty free-for-all directed to Faunus and based on ancient fertility celebrations.

LUSITANIA An imperial Roman province in Farther Spain.

LUTETIA PARISIORUM The principal city of the Parisii in the Roman province of Gallia Lugdunensis (that is, Gaul based on modern Lyons): modern Paris. It was a favourite town of Julian and he was proclaimed emperor there in A.D. 360.

LYCAON King of Arcadia, son of Pelasgus, who sacrificed a child to Zeus in an attempt to ingratiate himself and was consequently, with all his sons except one, either struck dead by a thunderbolt or changed into a wolf.

LYCEUM The gymnasium in Athens called after the temple of Apollo Lyceus nearby where Aristotle actively discussed philosophy with the Peripatetics.

LYCIA An area in the south of Asia Minor.

LYCOMEDES King of the Dolopians in the island of Scyrus, whose daughter conceived Pyrrhus (Neoptolemus) by Achilles when Achilles was sent there by Thetis in the disguise of a girl so that he would not go to the Trojan war.

LYCURGUS Traditionally the initiator of the highly individualistic legal constitution of Sparta.

LYDIA An area of the central west coast of Asia Minor.

LYNCEUS The only one of the 50 sons of AEGYPTUS (whom see) who was not slaughtered on his wedding night, but was saved by Hyper-mnestra and became king of Argos after Danaus.

LYSANDER Victorious Spartan general and admiral, died 395 B.C.

LYSIPPUS Skilful sculptor of Sicyon, contemporary of Alexander the Great, who said that no painter but Apelles should take his portrait, no sculptor but Lysippus.

M

MACEDONIA The country north of Greece which, from the time of Alexander the Great until the Roman imperium, dominated the entire peninsula.

MACRINUS (MARCUS OPELLIUS MACRINUS) African praetorian prefect who had Caracalla assassinated and reigned for a year as emperor, A.D. 217–218.

MAECENAS (CAIUS CILNIUS MAECENAS) A confidant of Augustus and patron of Virgil and Horace, died 8 B.C.

MAGNENTIUS Roman emperor of the west A.D. 350–353.

MAIA Daughter of Atlas, eldest and loveliest of the Pleiades, mother of Hermes by Zeus.

MANES Those spirits of the dead whom the Romans worshipped as gods.

MANLIUS (MARCUS MANLIUS) Consul in Rome 392 B.C., in 387 became aware of a night assault by the Gauls from the cackling of the sacred geese on the Capitoline, and led a successful sortie.

MANTUA Regarded by Virgil as his birthplace.

MARATHON A plain 26 miles from Athens, enclosed by mountain and marshland, where the battle between the Persians and the Athenians was fought in 490 B.C.

MARIUS (CAIUS MARIUS) Soldier of humble origin who became renowned for his victories in Africa, became consul in 107 B.C. at the age of 50 and was consul successively from 104–100. Over a decade later he tried to return to power in rivalry with Sulla, marched on Rome and appointed himself consul for the seventh time in 86 B.C., and died almost immediately.

MARS An ancient Italian god of Sabine origin adopted by the Romans as god of war and identified with Ares.

MARSI A warlike tribe of central Italy.

MARSYAS A satyr in Phrygia who found the flute which Athene had abandoned because it distorted her beauty in the playing. He learned the instrument, challenged Apollo to a contest and, losing, was flayed alive for his presumption.

MARTIAL (MARCUS VALERIUS MARTIALIS) Occasionally obscene Latin epigrammatic poet, A.D. 40–104, who offended taste more by slavish flattery of the emperor Domitian.

MASINISSA A local king in north Africa who, siding with the Romans in the second Punic war, was made king of Numidia, married Sophonisba, and reigned for 50 creative years until his death in 149 B.C.

MASSILIA (in Greek, MASSALIA) A colony founded from Phocis c. 600 B.C., became a centre of commerce and Hellenism: modern Marseille.

MAURETANIA A country in north Africa, later a Roman province.

MAUSOLOS King of Caria 377–353 B.C., for an account of whose tomb see ARTEMISIA.

MARS AND VENUS.

MAXENTIUS Roman emperor A.D. 306–312, see LICINIUS.

MAXIMIANUS Roman emperor A.D. 286–305, ousted by GALERIUS MAXIMIANUS and his own son Maxentius in 305. He obeyed the order of Constantine to commit suicide in 310. Galerius Maximianus died in 311.

MAXIMINUS 1. Roman emperor A.D. 235–238. 2. Roman emperor 308–314, nephew of Galerius Maximianus, uneasy colleague of Licinius.

MAXIMUS (MAGNUS CLEMENS MAXIMUS) Roman emperor A.D. 383–388.

MEDEA Daughter of Aeëtes king of Colchis, became infatuated with Jason when he came to seek the golden fleece, aided him and fled with him to Greece, staying her father's pursuit by a ghoulish ploy (see APSYRTUS), in Iolcus rejuvenated Jason's father and cunningly got Pelias killed (see ACASTUS). Later Medea was abandoned by Jason and in revenge killed their children and his new wife.

MEDIA An important province of the Persian empire.

MEDIOLANUM The residence of the emperors of the west after A.D. 284: modern Milan.

MEDUSA See GORGONES.

MEGAERA See EUMENIDES.

MEGALOPOLIS A city of Arcadia deliberately formed in 371 B.C. by drafting the inhabitants of 38 villages nearby.

MELEAGER Son of Oeneus king of Calydon, Argonaut and participant in the boar hunt, where he fell in love with Atalanta.

MELETUS The former accuser of SOCRATES, whom see.

MELISSA The nymph who discovered honey.

MELITA Island colonised from Phoenicia *c.* 1000 B.C., in the hands of Carthage for three centuries until 218 B.C. when it became a Roman protectorate: modern Malta.

MELPOMENE The Muse of tragedy.

MEMNON King of Aethiopia who fought at Troy for his uncle, Priam. He was the son of Eos, who had cajoled from Hephaestus special armour for him to wear, and wearing this he killed Antilochus but was killed by Achilles. Zeus soothed Eos by making Memnon immortal, and various columns over the ancient world are associated with him in a cult emphasising immortality.

MEMPHIS Principal city of Egypt after the eclipse of Thebes.

MENANDER Comic playwright of Athens, 342–291 B.C., drowned while swimming in the Piraeus.

MENELAUS Younger brother of AGAMEMNON, whom see, the husband of Helen whose elopement with Paris started the Trojan war. Outside Troy he was only prevented from killing Paris by the application of magic from Aphrodite. He finally took Helen home with him to Sparta.

MERCURIUS (MERCURY) The Roman god of commerce who gradually was assigned all the attributes of the Greek Hermes.

MESOPOTAMIA The land between the rivers Tigris and Euphrates.

MESSALINA (VALERIA MESSALINA) Profligate wife of Claudius and mother of Britannicus. In A.D. 48, with considered but misjudged recklessness, she publicly married and equally publicly bedded the gigolo Caius Silius while Claudius was at Ostia. It seems to have been a complete revelation to the emperor of his wife's unrealised character, and Claudius had her put to death.

MESSANA Sicilian town of the Siculi, originally called Zancle because of the sickle-shape of its harbour, colonised from Chalcis *c.* 725 B.C. using

MIDAS, WITH APOLLO AND PAN.

settlers already in Sicily and Cumae, taken over by Samians from Miletus in Caria after the destruction of that town by the Persians in 494 B.C., but shortly afterwards captured by Greeks from MESSENIA (which see) darting over the strait from Rhegium (modern Reggio) under the leadership of Axaxilas, who changed the name of the settlement to Messana or Messene. It was destroyed by the Carthaginians in 396 B.C., rebuilt by Dionysius tyrant of Syracuse, but taken over in 282 by Mamertini mercenaries of AGATHOCLES, whom see, who slaughtered the males, possessed the females, and re-named the town Mamertina. The Mamertini called on Rome to protect them from Carthage, and the city became the overt cause of the first Punic war. From that time Messana (modern Messina) became a favoured Roman protectorate.

MESSENIA The south-west area of the Peloponnesus, oppressed by Sparta for 300 years, a state of tension that was responsible for much Messenian emigration, see MESSANA.

METIS The supreme spirit of mild wisdom, daughter of Oceanus and Tethys, the first wife of Zeus, who devoured her in self-aggrandisement (see ATHENA).

MIDAS Son of GORDIUS, whom see, and king of Phrygia, renowned for the Midas touch from which – since he could not eat gold – he was saved by Dionysus. When Midas was appointed judge of a musical contest between Pan on the flute and Apollo on the lyre, and he decided in favour of Pan, Apollo gave him the ears of an ass, which he managed to conceal under his Phrygian cap from everyone except the servant who cut his hair.

MILETUS A magnificent city, state and imperial centre on the west coast of Asia Minor, destroyed by the Persians in 494 B.C. and later by Alexander the Great.

MILO (MILON) An athlete from Croton, six times winning the wrestling at the Olympic games and six times at the Pythian – an astonishing feat when it is considered that they spanned over 20 years – who distinguished himself as a soldier in 511 B.C. (The *Venus de Milo* comes from Melos, the island in the Cyclades group encircling Delos.)

MILTIADES Athenian general, *c.* 540–489 B.C., at one time tyrant of the Thracian Chersonese in succession to his uncle Miltiades, played a controversial part in the war of Darius I against the Scythians, won the battle of Marathon against the Persians in 490, used his prestige to mount a private belligerent expedition against Paros and was impeached, but died in prison.

MINERVA An Italian goddess of handicrafts gradually assimilated by the Romans with Athena.

MINOS 1. Son of Zeus and Europa, king of Crete, after his death a judge in the land of Hades. 2. Grandson of the preceding, king of Crete who exacted the sacrifice from Athenians to the Minotaur, husband of PASIPHAЁ, whom see, eventually killed by DAEDALUS, whom see.

MITHRAS Asian god of light and wisdom, worshipped in secret and only by men, with ceremonies including blood-baptism, who became a peculiar cult of the Roman legions.

MITHRIDATES The name of many kings of Pontus on the Black Sea, notably Mithridates VI, 120–63 B.C., who warred against the Romans in Asia Minor, the Aegean and in Greece, but who caused such misery at home that he was finally put down by his own son, Pharnaces.

MNEMOSYNE The personification of memory, daughter of Uranus and mother of the Muses by Zeus.

MOIRAE The FATES, which see.

MOMUS The Greek god of satirical censure.

MONETA An aspect of Juno as the protectress of money.

MOPSUS Son of Apollo and Manto, a diviner who proved himself a better seer than CALCHAS, whom see.

MORPHEUS One of the sons of the god of sleep, sending dreams of

MNEMOSYNE.

ONE OF THE MUSES, ERATO.

human beings, whereas his brothers Ikelos and **Phanta sos portrayed** beasts and objects.

MORS (the Greek THANATOS) The personification o f death.

MUSES Originally the Greek goddesses of song, the daughters of Zeus and Mnemosyne, later the nine deities of the arts: Clio, history; Euterpe, lyric poetry; Thalia, comedy; Melpomene, tragedy; Terpsichore, choral dance and song; Erato, erotic poetry; Polymnia, the sublime hymn; Urania, astronomy; Calliope, epic poetry.

MYCENAE An ancient town in Argolis known to have existed from 3000 B.C., particularly flourishing between 1400 and 1150 B.C., in Hellenic days subsidiary to ARGOS, which see.

MYRMIDONES The people subject to Achilles who accompanied him from Phthiotis in Thessaly to Troy.

MYRON Greek sculptor, working in the mid-5th century B.C., specialising in bronze, who cast the original of the extant copy of the Discobulus.

MYTILENE The principal city of Lesbos.

N

NAIADES The Nymphs of fresh water.

NARCISSUS The handsome son of Cephissus and Liriope for love of whom Echo pined and died, in consequence of which Nemesis condemned him to fall in love with his image in a pool, and he, too, pined and died, changing into the flower.

NAUSICAA The daughter of Alcinous king of the Phaeacians who discovered Odysseus, shipwrecked and naked in Scheria.

NAXOS 1. An island in the Aegean. 2. A town on the east coast of Sicily founded by settlers from Chalcis in 735 B.C.

NEAPOLIS City in Campania founded by Chalcideans from the nearby colony of Cumae in 600 B.C., modern Naples.

NECESSITAS (Greek ANANKE) The irresistible goddess who posts up the decrees of Fate with brass nails.

NELEUS Son of Poseidon, twin of PELIAS, whom see, ejected from the joint throne of Iolcus by Pelias, became king of Pylos, had 12 sons, all of whom except Nestor were killed by Heracles.

NEMEA Valley in Argolis where Heracles slew the Nemean lion.

NEREID.

NIKE, OR VICTORIA.

NEMESIS Originally a balancing goddess, dealing good fortune to those over-oppressed as well as the reverse. Later exclusively concerned with punishment of crime.

NEOPTOLEMUS (sometimes PYRRHUS, of the fair hair) Son of Deidamia by Achilles. Arrived late in Troy, was in the wooden horse, killed Priam and was rewarded with Andromache. He was eventually killed by Orestes.

NEPOS See CORNELIUS NEPOS.

NEPTUNUS A pale Roman version of Poseidon, unappreciated since the Romans were not a seafaring nation.

NEREIS Any of the 50 daughters of Nereus and Doris. The Nereids were Nymphs associated only with the Mediterranean, distinct from the Oceanides.

NEREUS The old man of the sea, son of Pontus and Gaea.

NERO (NERO CLAUDIUS CAESAR) Son of CNAEUS DOMITIUS AHENOBARBUS and AGRIPPINA, whom see, born A.D. 37, by his mother's machinations succeeded CLAUDIUS, whom see, as emperor in 54, murdered his half-brother Britannicus, his mother and his wife and consolidated the corruption of his regime, survived the great fire of Rome in 64 and subsequent conspiracies, killed himself *in extremis* in A.D. 68.

NERVA (MARCUS COCCEIUS NERVA) Roman emperor A.D. 96–98.

NESTOR Only surviving son of NELEUS, whom see, king of Pylos, was an old man at the siege of Troy having participated previously in the fight between the Lapiths and the Centaurs and in the voyage of the Argo.

NIKE (Roman VICTORIA) the goddess of victory, daughter of the Titan Pallas and the Nymph Styx.

NICIAS Wealthy Athenian general *c.* 470–413 B.C.

NINUS The founder of, and the alternative name of, Nineveh.

NIOBE Daughter of Tantalus, wife of AMPHION, whom see, boasted injudiciously of the large number of her children to Leto, whose children Artemis and Apollo promptly shot all Niobe's children with arrows. Zeus changed Niobe into a stone on Mount Sipylon, which continued to shed tears.

NISUS King of Megara whose life depended on a lock of red hair on the top of his head. Megara was being besieged by Minos, with whom Scylla, the daughter of Nisus, had fallen in love. She plucked out the lock of hair and Nisus was overcome. Minos drowned her by making her a figure-head in his ship. Alternatively, Nisus was changed into a sea-eagle and Scylla into an edible bird which he pursued.

NOTUS The south-west wind, Auster.

N O X The presence of Night, daughter of Chaos.

NUMA POMPILIUS The second king of Rome, said to have lived from 715 to 673 B.C.

NUMIDIA Country, originally peopled by nomads, in Africa to the south of Carthage.

NYMPHS Daughters of Zeus, but not immortal, living in the Ocean, Oceanides; the Mediterranean, Nereides; fresh water, Naiades; mountains, Oreades; glens, Napaeae; and trees, Dryades and Hamadryades.

O

OCEANIDES The nymphs of the western Ocean.

OCEANUS Son of Uranus and Ge (Heaven and Earth), husband of Tethys, lord of the water encircling the whole world, because of the presence of Asia only recognisable in the west, but faithfully believed to embrace the world, if only so that Helios could be ferried back to the east again at every nightfall.

OCTAVIUS See AUGUSTUS.

ODYSSEUS Son of Laertes and later his successor as king of Ithaca, husband of Penelope, the Greek hero in the Trojan war whose long wanderings homewards are the theme of Homer's *Odyssey* and other works.

OEDIPUS Son of Laius king of Thebes, exposed on Mount Cithaeron at birth because his father believed an oracle that a son would kill him; reared by king Polybus of Corinth; Oedipus being told by the Delphic oracle that he would kill his father and couple with his mother, he travelled away from Corinth, but fell in with Laius and killed him in a brawl. He came to Thebes, solved the riddle of the Sphinx, and was rewarded with the hand of the queen, who was his mother Jocasta. They had four children. Thebes was visited with the plague and an oracle declared that it would endure until the murderer of Laius was expelled. Another seer revealed that this man was Oedipus. Jocasta hanged herself, Oedipus blinded himself and became a vagrant, accompanied by his daughter Antigone. He died at Colonus.

OENONE The wife of Paris before the rape of Helen, she killed herself when Paris died.

OLYMPIA A plain in Elis with a grove dedicated to Zeus where the quadrennial Olympic Games were held.

OLYMPUS 1. The mountain range separating Thessaly and Macedonia, said to be the home of the gods. 2. A mountain range in north-west Asia Minor.

OPS Roman goddess of plenty, the wife of Saturnus.

ORBILIUS PUPILLUS The schoolmaster who repeatedly flogged the poet Horace.

OREADES Nymphs of the glens.

ORESTES Son of AGAMEMNON and CLYTAEMNESTRA, whom see. Clytaemnestra would have murdered him as well as his father, but Electra saved him and eventually he took revenge by killing his mother. But he went mad and fled, pursued by the Furies, until a court convened by Athena calmed him by acquittal.

ORION A giant hunter who was blinded but recovered his sight by exposing his eyeballs to the rising sun. Eos then conceived a passion for him and carried him off, but Artemis shot him with her arrow. He was placed among the stars.

ORPHEUS Traditionally to the Greeks, a master of poetry and song. They believed him to be a son of Calliope who possessed a lyre which was the gift of Apollo and on which he played so expressively that he charmed beasts, rocks and trees. He went on the Argonaut adventure and on his return married Eurydice in Thrace. She died of a snake-bite and he followed her into the land of Hades, using his lyre to such effect that he won back his wife on condition that he did not look at her until they were in the upper world. In a moment of loving concern he broke this condition, and she was claimed back. In his grief Orpheus slighted some women indulging in a Bacchanalia and they tore him to pieces.

OSIRIS The Egyptian god, husband of Isis, originally the representation of the dead Pharaoh.

OSSA A mountain in northern Thessaly.

OSTIA The harbour at the mouth of the river Tiber.

OSTRACISM In Athenian practice, banishment without loss of civil rights.

OTHO (MARCUS SALVIUS OTHO) A friend of Nero, who seduced his wife and gave him a post in Africa to get rid of him in A.D. 58, when he was 26 years old. On Nero's death in 68 he claimed the empire but could not hold it, ruled only for three months and committed suicide after military defeat in A.D. 69.

OVID (PUBLIUS OVIDIUS NASO) Latin poet, 43 B.C.–A.D. 17, educated at Rome and Athens in law and rhetoric. He took an undistinguished administrative post and began to write poetry, including the polished eroticism of the *Ars Amatoria*, which in the year A.D. 8 was made the pretext for his banishment by Augustus to Tomis on the Black Sea (modern Costanza) where he died.

PQ

PACUVIUS (MARCUS PACUVIUS) Both a tragic playwright and a painter, born at Brundisium (Brindisi) *c.* 220 B.C., flourished in Rome and died at Tarentum 130 B.C.

PADUS The river Po.

PAEAN Originally a hymn to Apollo as the Healer, later an artistic tribute to a god or mortal.

PAESTUM A town in Lucania colonised from Sybaris in the south in the 6th century B.C., famous then for the roses that grew there, and now for the Doric temples which remain.

PALAESTINA In the original Hebrew, the land of the Philistines, later called by the Romans Judaea.

PALAMEDES A Greek hero at Troy renowned for guile; later represented as the joint-inventor of the alphabet and many technical innovations.

PALATINUS The Palatine Hill in Rome.

PALLADIUM An ancient image of Pallas Athene at Troy, on the integrity of which the city depended. It was taken by Odysseus and Diomedes. But the Romans believed that Aeneas brought it safely to Italy where it later safeguarded Rome.

PAN A god of flocks and herds native to Arcadia, but later made the son of Hermes. He invented the flute and was as casually amorous as a god of fertility should be.

PANATHENAEA The yearly Athenian festival, culminating every fourth year in the Great Panathenaea, depicted on the frieze of the Parthenon.

PANDORA The first woman on earth, made from earth at the command of Zeus by Hephaestus, and destined to bring woe to the future human race as a reprisal for the feat of Prometheus in stealing fire from heaven. She brought from Olympus a box containing all the ills of the world, which escaped when the casket was opened, except that Hope alone remained.

PANTHEON The temple in the Campus Martius at Rome originally built by Marcus Agrippa in 27–25 B.C., destroyed by fire and rebuilt by Hadrian.

PAPHOS The name of two towns in Cyprus, one on the coast, the other inland, Aphrodite's great temple being at the latter.

PARIS Second son of Priam and Hecuba of Troy, chosen to judge between the beauty of Hera, Aphrodite and Athena as the result of an intrigue by Eris, the goddess of strife. His choice of APHRODITE (whom see) brought the wrath of Hera and Athena on Troy. Aphrodite had promised him the seduction of Helen as a prize, and Paris carried her off from Menelaus. Paris was eventually saved from death at the hands of Menelaus, but shot with an arrow directed by Hermes.

PARNASSUS The high point of the mountain range north of Delphi, the seat of Apollo and the Muses.

PAROS An island in the Aegean famous for its marble.

PARTHENON The temple to Athena on the Acropolis of Athens inspired by Pericles and built by Ictinus and Callicrates with sculptures by Phidias.

PARTHIA A country south-east of the Caspian inhabited by a warlike race famous for their skill as cavalry and a knack of shooting behind them during a tactical retreat.

PASIPHAË Daughter of Helios, wife of Minos, mother by him of Phaedra and others, and by the bull of the Minotaur, who mounted her in the construction designed by Daedalus.

PATROCLUS The friend of Achilles who took command of the Myrmidons at Troy while his chief sulked in his tent.

PAULINUS (CAIUS SUETONIUS PAULINUS) Governor of Britain A.D. 59–62 who suppressed the revolt of Boudicca.

PAUSANIUS 1. Spartan commander of the allied Greek forces at the battle of Plataea, 479 B.C. He was accused of aiming to become tyrant of Greece and died 470. 2. A Greek explorer and geographer of about A.D. 150.

PAX (Greek IRENE) The Roman goddess of peace.

PELASGI The ancient inhabitants of Greece.

PELEUS The son of Aeacus, for whose adventures see ACASTUS.

PELIAS The brother of NELEUS, whom see, and usurper of the throne due to JASON, whom see.

PELOPONNESUS The southern peninsula of Greece.

PELION A range of high mountains in Thessaly. On the path to the summit there was the cave of Chiron. At the summit lay the temple of Zeus Actaeus.

PELOPS Grandson of Zeus, son of Tantalus, king of Phrygia, from which land he was expelled, and he came to Elis and married Hippodameia, the daughter of the king Oenamaus, whom he later succeeded. Pelops had one shoulder of ivory (and his descendants had the genetic particularity of a white shoulder) which had been occasioned when his

PANDORA, AND HER BOX.

father Tantalus, a man of joking disposition who normally could take any liberties with the gods, invited the gods to dinner and served them as a dish his own son Pelops, cut up and boiled. The omniscient gods did not touch this course of the meal, except Demeter, who was preoccupied with grief for the loss of Persephone and absent-mindedly ate the shoulder. The gods instructed Hermes to put the flesh back into a kettle and boil it, and when Clotho, the spinner among the Fates, took it out again, Pelops was restored and living except that he lacked one shoulder, and this Demeter replaced in ivory. When Pelops sought Hippodameia as a bride, Oenamaus said that the rule of the house was that a suitor carried off his daughter, but was to be pursued by Oenamaus in his chariot, and if the king caught up with the suitor he should kill him: which had already happened thirteen times. Pelops agreed, but bribed the king's charioteer, Myrtilus, to take out the pins securing the chariot wheels. This was done, and Oenamaus was thrown out and killed. Later Pelops threw Myrtilus into the sea. Either Oenamaus or Myrtilus or both pronounced a powerful dying curse on Pelops and his progeny, but for the moment he thrived as king of Pisa in Elis and injected new glory into the Olympic Games organised from there. Pelops had three sons, Atreus, Thyestes and Chrysippus, of whom the last was his favourite and was murdered by Atreus and Thyestes at the suggestion of Hippodameia – or by Hippodameia with the connivance of the others – and thus began the tragic sequence noted under ATREUS.

PENATES The household gods of the Romans, spirits envisaged as residing in the central store-cupboard of the home.

PENELOPE Wife of Odysseus of Ithaca and mother of Telemachus, faithfully waited twenty years for her husband's return from Troy, putting off her numerous suitors by working daily on a shroud, and nightly unpicking it. Other versions of the story than Homer's give her a more inconstant character.

PENEUS God of the principal river in Thessaly, a son of Oceanus and Tethys, father of Daphne and Cyrene.

PENTATHLON An athletic contest in running, jumping, wrestling, and throwing the discus and the javelin.

PENTHESILEA Daughter of Ares, queen of the Amazons, she came to aid Troy after the death of Hector and was killed by Achilles, who uncharacteristically mourned her, provoking the ridicule of Thersites, for which Achilles killed Thersites, whose kinsman Diomedes then defiled the body of Penthesilia.

PENTHEUS Succeeded his grandfather Cadmus as king of Thebes and resisted the introduction of the worship of Dionysus, but at the height of a Bacchanalia which he was spying on from a tree he was torn to pieces by the frenzied women, headed by his mother Agave and her sisters Ino and Autonoë.

PERDIX The nephew of DAEDALUS, whom see, and the inventor of the saw, the chisel and the compasses; for which presumption Daedalus jealously threw him from the Parthenon. By some accounts he fell to his death, by others Athena caught him and changed him into a partridge.

PERGAMUM 1. A poetical name for Troy. 2 A great city of Mysia in Asia Minor, 15 miles inland from the coast opposite Lesbos, eventually the capital of a powerful kingdom under Eumenes II (reigned 197–159 B.C.), who founded the famous library which rivalled Alexandria's.

PERICLES The greatest Athenian statesman, c. 495–429 B.C., came into the leadership of the more democratic party in Athens in opposition to Cimon, whom he prosecuted for the State, and Thucydides, whom he had ostracised. Living a highly political life, he was subject to constant harassment, but he successfully beautified Athens with public buildings including the Parthenon (447–432 B.C.). His military strategy for the Peloponnesian war, 431, was disastrously rejected and he died 429.

PERSEPHONE (PROSERPINA) Daughter of Zeus and Demeter, desired by Hades and eventually carried off by him to the savage grief of Demeter who constantly sought her, and was finally appeased by an Olympian compromise whereby Persephone (like the seed corn which is Demeter's most significant offspring) spends a part of the year below the surface of the earth and a part of the year above it.

PERSEPOLIS The capital of the Persian empire.

[167]

PHAËTHON.

PERSEUS Son of ZEUS and DANAË, whom see, exposed at sea with his mother immediately after being born, since the father of Danaë still feared that the infant would cause his death. In manhood Perseus had to perform the feat of securing the head of MEDUSA, whom see, after which he rescued ANDROMEDA whom see, and after many adventures accidentally killed his grandfather Acrisius with a discus.

PERSIS Persia.

PERTINAX (PUBLIUS HELVIUS PERTINAX) A sound general under the emperor Marcus Aurelius and his son Commodus, Pertinax was, on the death of Commodus, proclaimed emperor by the Praetorian Guard on the understanding that they would receive a substantial bonus for that favour. When the payment was not deemed high enough, the Guard murdered Pertinax and put the empire up for sale, A.D. 193.

PETRONIUS ARBITER Companion and master of ceremonies of the emperor Nero who opened his veins when accused of treason. He wrote the *Satyricon*, a witty and informatively vulgar picaresque tale.

PHAEDRA Daughter of Minos, second wife of Theseus, made a Potiphar's-wife accusation against her stepson Hippolytus, with fatal consequences, and later hanged herself.

PHAEDRUS Latin fabulist *c.* 15 B.C.–A.D. 50, born in Macedonia, has 97 fables extant.

PHAËTHON Son of Helios and Clymene, begged the use of the Sun-Chariot for a day, but drove it so inexpertly that Zeus killed him with a thunderbolt and transformed his mourning sisters into poplars dropping amber.

PHALARIS Tyrant of Acragas (Agrigentum), Sicily *c.* 570–554 B.C., noted for the cruelty with which he roasted victims alive in a brazen bull.

PHALERUM The harbour of Athens used principally before the construction of harbours in the Piraeus.

PHARSALUS Town in Thessaly where Caesar defeated Pompey 48 B.C.

[169]

PHARUS (PHAROS) The island off Alexandria joined to the shore by the mole of Alexander the Great and illuminated by the light-house of Ptolemy II.

PHIDIAS (PHEIDIAS) Athenian sculptor, *c.* 490 B.C. – 417 B.C., who designed the original models from which subordinate sculptors carved the figures on the frieze of the Parthenon. A worker in bronze, none of his original statues remain.

PHILEMON Phrygian husband of **BAUCIS**, whom see.

PHILIPPI City in Macedonia where Octavian and Antony defeated Brutus and Cassius in 42 B.C., and St Paul preached the gospel in Europe for the first time, A.D. 53.

PHILIPPUS The name of many kings of Macedonia, notably 1. Philip II, born 382 B.C., reigned 359-336, who unified and aggrandised Macedonia, fought and then conciliated Athens, persuaded the Greeks to unite and oppose Persia, but was assassinated before the expedition was organised and was succeeded by his son Alexander the Great; 2. Philip V, born 238 B.C., reigned 221-179, fought two wars with the Romans but was punitively defeated in 197.

PHILOCTETES A celebrated archer who inherited the bow and poisoned arrows of Heracles, a suitor of Helen who intended to participate in the war against Troy but staying *en route* on the island of Chryse received a snake-bite which later caused him to stink so much that he was left behind in Lemnos. In the tenth year of the war, an oracle declared that the struggle would not be won without him, he was fetched by Odysseus and Diomedes and was said to have killed Paris.

PHILOMELA Daughter of Pandion, king of Athens and sister of Procne, who was married to Tereus, king of Thrace, or king of the Thracians in Phocis. Tereus later lied that Procne was dead, sent for Philomela, ravished her and cut out her tongue. Philomela found a means of communicating her fate on a piece of embroidery which she sent to Procne, who served to Tyreus a dish containing the flesh of their son Itys. Tyreus chased the sisters with an axe. But he was changed into a hoopoe, or possibly a hawk, and Procne was changed into a nightingale and Philomela into a swallow, or possibly vice versa.

PHILOPOEMEN Called 'the last of the Greeks' in the sense of his eminence during the decline of Greece; born *c.* 253 B.C., revitalised Greek military glory and political influence, he was forced to drink poison after defeat in 182 B.C., but had re-established the status of Greece *vis-à-vis* Rome.

PHILOTAS *c.* 360–330 B.C., a friend of Alexander the Great, falsely accused of conspiracy against him and stoned to death by the troops.

PHILOXENUS Dithyrambic poet of Greece who spent some time after 400 B.C. in the court of Dionysius of Syracuse and produced a famous rejoinder to literary criticism when the tyrant asked him to revise a poem, and he said the only suitable revision would be to cross it out. For this he was sent to the slate quarries.

PHOCAEA The northernmost Ionian city on the west coast of Asia Minor, famous for having colonised Massilia (modern Marseilles).

PHOCIS A country round the Cephissus valley in Greece containing Parnassus and the Delphic Oracle.

PHOEBE Used for Artemis as the bright one, the moon, successor to Phoebus the sun.

PHOENICIA The coastal strip of Syria.

PHOENIX 1. The tutor of Achilles who had fled to Phthia after wooing his father's mistress in order to effect a reconciliation between his parents, and was forthwith cursed by his father. 2. The Egyptian bird which, after a life of 500 years, incinerated itself and simultaneously gave birth to a new phoenix.

PHORCYS A sea god, son of Pontus and Ge and father of the Gorgones and the Graeae.

PHRIXUS The brother of Helle, who was to be sacrificed to Zeus with his sister when Hermes intervened and gave their mother Nephele a flying ram with a golden fleece on which they were to escape. Helle fell off the ram into the Hellespont.

PHRYGIA The central and western area of Asia Minor, the inhabitants of which were progressively considered submissive and servile, although the characteristic conical Phrygian hat became identified as the cap of liberty.

PHRYNE A courtesan of Athens, *fl. c.* 340 B.C. who was both mistress and model to Apelles the painter and Praxiteles the sculptor.

PHTHIOTIS (PHTHIA) The area in south-west Thessaly from which Achilles came.

PICTI A Caledonian tribe who were observed by the Romans to paint their bodies.

PICUS In Latin culture, son of Saturnus and father of Faunus, a youth with the gift of prophecy who was in love with Pomona, was loved by Circe and, rejecting her, was changed into a woodpecker.

PIERIA The south-eastern strip of Macedonia, an early home of the Muses.

PIMPLEA A town in Pieria dedicated to the Muses.

PINDAR (PINDARUS) Lyric poet from Boeotia, 518–438 B.C., sometimes bowdlerising the old myths for the sake of morality, whose long poem *Epicinia* survives.

PIRAEUS The principal habour-site of Athens, five miles from the city.

PIRENE The fountain in Corinth where Bellerophon caught Pegasus.

PIRITHOUS Son of IXION, whom see and king of the Lapiths.

PHRIXUS AND HELLE.

With Theseus he resolved to carry off Persephone from the land of Hades, but both were seized by the king of the underworld and chained to a rock. Heracles later released Theseus but not Pirithous.

PISA The capital of Pisatis in Elis, very near Olympia, the inhabitants of which constantly disputed with the Eleans the sponsorship of the Olympic Games and were finally overcome in 572 B.C.

PISAE Modern Pisa.

PISISTRATUS Tyrant of Athens 560–527 B.C. but not continuously, a kinsman of Solon who did in fact prepare the state for democracy.

PISO (CNAEUS CALPURNIUS PISO) A libertine friend of Caesar and Crassus who was a collaborator in the Cataline conspiracy of 66 B.C. and was sent to a post in Spain, where he was murdered in 64.

PITTACUS Statesman, philosopher and poet of Mytilene, c. 650–570 B.C., who led a war against Athens and in later administration was famous for a law doubling the penalty for any offence committed during drunkenness.

PLATAEA A city in Boeotia, laid in ruins by Xerxes in 480 B.C. but the effective site of the battle in 479 when the Greeks defeated the Persians.

PLATO 1. An Athenian comic playwright who flourished between 428 and 389 B.C. 2. The Athenian philosopher, c. 429–347 B.C., became a disciple of Socrates in 409 and after his death in 399 briefly exiled himself and returned to teach at the Academy with two breaks to visit Dionysius in Syracuse. Apart from his continuously influential philosophy, his prose style is a classical mingling of the easy with the poetic.

PLAUTUS (TITUS MACCIUS PLAUTUS) Roman comic playwright, born in Umbria 254 B.C., wrote his first plays in Rome while employed in a bakery. In the next forty years until his death in 184 he wrote an unknown number of comedies, of which 21 authentic scripts survive.

PLEIADES The seven daughters of Atlas and Pleione, virgin companions of Artemis, pursued by Orion in Boeotia and changed into doves, then placed among the stars, and identified now as in the constellation Taurus.

PLINY (PLINIUS) 1. Pliny the Elder, GAIUS PLINIUS SECUNDUS, born at Comum (modern Como) A.D. 23, educated in Rome, served as a cavalry officer, retired at the age of 35 to take up advocacy and literature but under his friend Vespasian he was appointed to a number of successive colonial governorships. When admiral at Misenum, near Cumae, he went ashore to take closer scientific observations of the eruption of Vesuvius, 24 August A.D. 79, and was asphyxiated on the strand at Castellammare. His book on Natural History survives. 2. Pliny the Younger, GAIUS PLINIUS CAECILIUS SECUNDUS, born c. A.D. 61 at Comum and on his father's early death was adopted by his uncle, Pliny the Elder. At first a legal referee in property disputes, he took up political advocacy and featured in several notable trials indifferently as prosecutor or for the defence. In 103 he was appointed by Trajan as governor of Bithynia with special responsibility for reorganising the finances of the provinces, and the volume of letters he exchanged with the emperor on this subject is a prime historical source. There are also extant nine books of polished letters (re-written for publication) to his family and friends. He died between A.D. 110 and 113.

PLISTHENES Son of ATREUS, whom see, and father of Agamemnon and Menelaus.

PLOTINA (POMPEIA PLOTINA) Childless wife of Trajan who persuaded him to adopt her favourite, Hadrian. She died A.D. 121 and was consecrated as a goddess.

PLUTARCH (PLUTARCHUS) Biographer and philosopher, born and died (c. A.D. 46–120) in Boeotia but spent his middle years in Rome.

PLUTO The giver of wealth, a flattering reference to Hades.

PLUTUS The god of wealth.

PLUVIUS The rain-maker, a term used for Jupiter at sacrifices during periods of drought.

POLLIO (ASINIUS POLLIO) A Roman politician, playwright and historian, 76 B.C.–A.D. 5, who influentially acted as mediator between Octavian and Antony and was patron and friend of Virgil and Horace.

POLLIO (VEDIUS POLLIO) An intimate of Augustus, died 15 B.C., notorious for his practice of throwing slaves who displeased him into a pond to feed his lampreys, and ultimately himself.

POLLUX The Roman version of Polydeuces, one of the Dioscuri.

POLYBIUS Greek historian of Rome, c. 203–120 B.C., personally witnessed in the same year, 146, the destruction of Carthage and of Corinth by the Romans, and ended his 40-volume history at that point.

POLYCLETUS A Greek sculptor, fl. 452–412 B.C., a slightly younger contemporary of Phidias but apparently entirely uninfluenced by him.

POLYDORUS Youngest son of Priam, killed by Achilles.

POLYGNOTUS An Athenian painter, fl. 475–447 B.C.

POLYHYMNIA The Muse of the sublime hymn.

POLYPHEMUS The one-eyed Cyclops, son of Poseidon, who crushed Acis to death when Galatea showed her preference for him, and devoured the companions of Odysseus before the hero put out his eye.

POLYXENA The daughter of Priam and Hecuba with whom Achilles was said to be in love and who was killed on the tomb of her father by NEOPTOLEMUS, whom see, the son of Achilles, when the shade of Achilles appeared and demanded that sacrifice.

POMONA The Roman goddess of fruit trees.

POMPEIA Married Caesar in 67 B.C. Because Clodius smuggled himself into their home, not necessarily for seduction but to observe the secret women's rites in the ceremonial mysteries of the Bona Dea, she was divorced in 61 because 'Caesar's wife had to be above suspicion'.

POMPEII A city of Campania, now two miles inland but a seaside resort in A.D. 79 when it was overcome by ash during the great eruption of Vesuvius.

POMPEY (CNAEUS POMPEIUS MAGNUS) Roman general and statesman, was born in 106 B.C. and served in the army before allying himself with Sulla in the war against the Marian party after 84. After his victories in Africa he was given a triumph in 81 and the title Magnus. Consul in 70 he became a popular hero for his democratic measures. Between 66 and 62 he waged successful war in the east against Mithridates and took Jerusalem. In 60 he formed a triumvirate with Caesar and Crassus and in 59 married Caesar's daughter Julia, but her death in 54 signalled the end of his relationship with Caesar. When Caesar crossed the Rubicon in 49 Pompey fled to Greece, where Caesar ultimately caught up with him and defeated him at Pharsalus in 48. He was killed in Alexandria later that year by agents of Ptolemy and his head was brought to Rome, but Caesar refused to look at it and executed the murderers.

PONTUS The region along the north-east stretches of Asia Minor by the Black Sea, politically important for the establishment there of a kingdom which was most influential under Mithridates VI, whom Pompey finally defeated.

PONTUS Is also used specifically for Pontus Euxinus, the Black Sea.

PORCIA (Shakespearean PORTIA) The wife of Marcus Junius Brutus, whom she married secondly after the consul Marcus Bibulus, an enthusiastic supporter of his republican principles in wishing to end the autocracy of Julius Caesar.

PORPHYRY (PORPHYRIUS) A Greek scholar and critic, c. A.D. 232–305, an editor of Plotinus but now known best as the author of a treatise against the Christian religion which was ordered to be publicly burnt (but not until A.D. 448, on the orders of the emperor Theodosius II).

POSEIDON.

PORSENA (PORSENNA : LARS PORSENA) King of Clusium in Etruria who marched on Rome to restore Tarquinius Superbus but was said to have withdrawn some time after the rearguard action involving HORATIUS COCLES, whom see.

POSEIDON Son of Cronus and Rhea, god of the Mediterranean ruling from a palace under the sea near Aegae in Euboea. Father of Triton and others by his wife Amphitrite, but his busy amours produced a vast progeny elsewhere. Although as 'human' in his weaknesses as Zeus in this respect, and occasionally more frighteningly petulant, he never acquired the genuine majesty which his brother developed.

POSTUMUS (MARCUS CASSIANUS LATINIUS POSTUMUS) Gallienus' commander on the Rhine, he proclaimed himself as independent emperor of Gaul in A.D. 259, issuing his own coinage from Cologne and eventually commanding territory as far as Britain and Spain. He was murdered by his own troops in 267 when he forbade them to sack Moguntiacum (modern Maintz) after its capture.

PRAXITELES Athenian sculptor working probably from 364 B.C. Carved an extant *Hermes* and a highly regarded *Aphrodite*, and excelled in portraying the draped female.

PRIAM (PRIAMUS) Son of Laomedon and king of Troy after being ransomed from Heracles by his sister Hesione. Hecuba was his second wife and said to be the mother of 19 of his 50 sons. Militarily his only intervention in the war around Troy was as an old man begging the body of his son Hector. At the fall of the city he was killed by Pyrrhus, son of Achilles.

PRIAPUS Son of Dionysus and Aphrodite, a god of fertility, given grotesque genitals by HERA, whom see, regarded less as a god to pray to than as a comic garden gnome whose statue in the rockery could raise a laugh and do no harm.

PROBUS (MARCUS AURELIUS PROBUS) Roman emperor A.D. 276–282.

PROCNE Sister of PHILOMELA, whom see.

PROCRUSTES Nickname (meaning 'the Stretcher') of a robber in the territory of Theseus who used to fasten his victims on a bed. If they were short, he stretched their limbs until they fitted, if they were tall he chopped their limbs to trim them. Theseus killed him.

PROETUS Twin brother of ACRISIUS, whom see, father of Lysippe, Iphinoë and Iphianassa, all of whom went mad, and spread their affliction throughout Argus, possibly after attendance at a Dionysian orgy.

PROMETHEUS Son of the Titan Iapetus and Clymene, brother of Atlas, Menoetius and Epimetheus. He benefitted mankind by stealing fire from heaven, but the result was the arrival of PANDORA, whom see, and the chaining of Prometheus to a rock on Caucasus where in the daytime an eagle pecked his liver, which during the night was restored – an interesting early anatomical detail, since the liver is the only human organ which renews itself.

PROPERTIUS (SEXTUS PROPERTIUS) Roman poet born c. 51 B.C. who began early to write most perceptive love poetry, much extant, which brought him to the notice of Maecenas.

PROPONTIS The Sea of Marmora, encountered (by the Greeks) 'before the Pontus', that is, west of the Black Sea.

PROPYLAEA A porch leading to a temple precinct as at the Acropolis of Athens.

PROSERPINA The Latin version of Persephone.

PROTAGORAS A philosopher of Athens, c. 485-415 B.C., the first to call himself a Sophist and the first to set himself up as a professional teacher, inculcating 'self-help' allied with gentlemanly conduct and wide cultural knowledge. It was a good augury for educators that this original public schoolmaster made, said Plato, more money than the dozen foremost sculptors of his time, including Phidias. He founded his faith in man and had a good-humoured scepticism about the gods (but not about the values they sometimes represented), but this agnosticism is said to have led to his impeachment in Athens for impiety, and a sentence variously recorded as banishment or the burning of one of his books.

PROTEUS The original old man of the sea. A fish-tailed son of Poseidon based on Pharos, the island off the Nile delta. The mythological personification of the sacred and oracular king of ancient times. The petitioner could 'have sight of Proteus rising from the sea' surrounded by his flock of seals at noontime, when it was his custom to come ashore and sleep in the shade. He had to be held very tightly before he would deliver the truth, and he resisted by constantly changing his shape.

PROTOGENES A painter of Rhodes, *fl.* 332–300 B.C., subsisting in poverty until on a brief visit to Athens the great artist Apelles publicly valued his work at 50 talents a picture, and the Rhodians paid up.

PRUDENTIUS A Spaniard born A.D. 343 who came to Rome and developed as the first considerable Latin poet of Christianity. Some of his work survives.

PSYCHE The soul, a fairly late conception in Greek thought, developed as the personification of a beautiful mortal virgin whose purity so exasperated Aphrodite that she told Eros to inspire her with love for the most contemptible of men. But Eros fell in love with her. The affair went unhappily, and Psyche wandered away and became a slave of Aphrodite and was constantly humiliated. But Eros continued his love and finally convinced Aphrodite that Psyche had been purged, or purified, more than enough. Psyche was made immortal and permanently united with Eros.

PTOLEMY (PTOLEMAEUS) The name of all the Macedonian kings of Egypt from Ptolemy I, *c.* 367–282 B.C., who founded the library at Alexandria and began a strong cultural tradition in his family. Ptolemy XIII, born 63 B.C., married his sister Cleopatra in 51 when he was 12 and she was 19, and made her joint ruler, but soon banished her. In 48 he was forced by Julius Caesar to admit her again to joint kingship. He rebelled and was drowned in the Nile in 47, and Caesar married Cleopatra to another of her brothers, then aged 12, who became Ptolemy XIV but was murdered by Cleopatra in 44, when Caesarion, the son of Julius Caesar and Cleopatra, became joint ruler with her as Ptolemy XV at the age of 13. He was killed by Octavian (Augustus) in 30 shortly after the ritual suicide of Cleopatra, and the line ended.

PUTEOLI An important sea port in Campania, the *entrepôt* for commerce with Egypt and Spain, modern Pozzuoli.

PYGMALION King of Cyprus who sculpted the figure of a woman in ivory and fell in love with it. At his request Aphrodite gave the statue life, and as Galatea she bore a daughter, Paphos, to Pygmalion.

PYLADES Son of the king of Phocis, contracted a deep friendship with Orestes, helped him murder his mother Clytaemnestra and later married Electra, the sister of Orestes.

PYLOS In Messenia, western Peloponnesus, the safest harbour in Greece which the Athenians successfully held against the Spartans in 425 B.C.

PYRRHO (PYRRHON) Greek philosopher, *c*. 360–270 B.C., who founded the school of the Sceptics but wrote no work himself.

PYRRHUS 1. NEOPTOLEMUS, whom see. 2. King of Epirus who never won a lasting victory. Born 319 B.C., after confused dynastic fortunes succeeded 297, had a showy but ineffective confrontation with Macedon 290–283, invaded Italy and defeated the Romans at Heraclea, 280 and Beneventum, 275, in the meantime almost, but not quite, expelling the Carthaginians from Sicily, retired to Epirus from Beneventum and began a fresh war against Macedon, killed in the streets of Argos 272.

PYTHAGORAS Greek philosopher, astronomer and mathematician famous for his belief in the transmigration of souls, emigrated to Magna Graecia, southern Italy, *c*. 531 B.C. and taught in the Greek cities there.

PYTHON The serpent which emerged from the mud after the Flood (see DEUCALION) and lived in the caves of Parnassus. It was killed by Apollo, four days after his birth, in the shrine of the oracle at Delphi, and the Pythian Games were instituted in its name, but to the glory of Apollo.

QUINTILIANUS (MARCUS FABIUS QUINTILIANUS)

Roman rhetorician born in Spain *c.* A.D. 37, practised in Rome from 68, later abandoned advocacy and became a paid professor of rhetoric. His great manual of oratory (*c.* A.D. 95) and three authentic speeches survive.

R

REGULUS 1. MARCUS ATILIUS REGULUS, consul 267 B.C., 256 B.C. Invaded Africa and in 255 was defeated by the Carthaginians, later dying in captivity. 2. MARCUS AQUILIUS REGULUS, flourished second half of 1st century A.D., an informer and later a ranting prosecutor named by the younger Pliny as the dirtiest blackguard on two legs.

REMUS See ROMULUS.

RHADAMANTHUS The son of Zeus and Europa, brother of Minos of Crete, a judge of the dead in the land of Hades.

RHEA The goddess who is the Great Mother in almost all ancient religions: in Greek mythology the daughter of Uranus and Ge (Heaven and Earth). She married her brother Cronus, the son of the same union. Cronus had maimed and cast down his father Uranus, who with his dying breath prophesied that the same fate would befall Cronus. Accordingly Cronus methodically swallowed his children as they were born to Rhea: Hestia, Demeter, Hera, Hades and Poseidon. When Rhea gave birth to Zeus, at midnight on Mount Lycaeus in Arcadia, she gave him swiftly to Mother Earth, her own mother, who concealed him in Crete and had him brought up by three nymphs (see AMALTHEA). Meanwhile Rhea gave Cronus a stone wrapped in swaddling clothes, telling him that this was Zeus, and he swallowed it. Zeus grew up in Ida and Rhea later got him the post of cup-bearer to Cronus. She prescribed a mixed

RHEA.

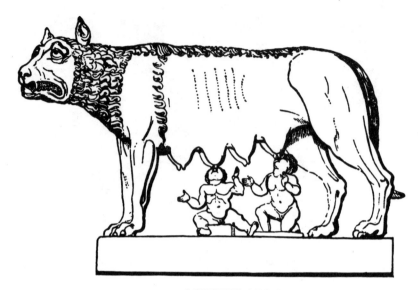

ROMULUS AND REMUS.

drink which Zeus gave to Cronus, who promptly vomited up his five
eldest children, all alive (and the stone, which was set up at Delphi).
Poseidon, Hades and Zeus then warred against Cronus and the Titans,
and triumphed after ten years, Zeus knocking Cronus out with a
thunderbolt and banishing him to Tartarus – or possibly a British island
in the west.

RHEA SILVIA The mother of ROMULUS, whom see.

RHEGIUM Town on the Fretum Siculum (Strait of Messina) founded
c. 720 B.C. by Greeks from Chalcis, later joined by Messenians, destroyed
by Dionysius 387 B.C. and captured by the Mamertines (see MESSANA)
who held it for ten years from 280 and treated its inhabitants exactly
as they had abused the Messinese, restored by the Romans after they had
recovered from the invasion of Pyrrhus, and thereafter a favoured Roman
protectorate (always Greek-speaking). Modern Reggio di Calabria.

RHENUS The river Rhine, first crossed by Roman armies by Julius
Caesar advancing from Gaul over a bridge of boats near Cologne.

RHODOPE A high mountain range in Thrace sacred to Dionysus.

RHODOPIS A famous prostitute, originally a Thracian slave-girl
owned by the same master as Aesop when he was a slave, living on Samos
in the 6th century B.C. The girl, then named Doricha, was sold to a
Samian whoremaster who set her up in a brothel in Naucratis the busy
Greek-orientated seaport in the Nile delta which was thriving long before
Alexandria. There she was seen by Charaxus, the merchant brother of
the woman poet Sappho, who fell in love with her (which irked Sappho)
and paid a vast sum to buy her out of slavery but did not release her from
prostitution, and the rosy-cheeked beauty continued to make a regular
fortune for herself and her pimp in Naucratis.

RHODES (RHODUS) (RHODOS) The most easterly island of the
Carpathian sea, named after Rhodos the daughter of Poseidon and
Aphrodite, settled by Dorian Greeks fairly early in the first millennium
B.C., always a prosperous maritime, commercial and imperial state until

it became a very junior partner of Rome after 167 B.C. The city of Rhodes (but not Lindus) was ruined in an earthquake in A.D. 155.

ROME Originally a federation of Latin and Sabine shepherds' settlements at the top of the seven hills, later admitting Etruscans to command them, but after the expulsion of Tarquinius Superbus in 510 B.C. developing as a distinct and characteristic state concerned to unite Latium, subdue Etruria and control first Italy, then the Mediterranean, particularly rival commercial imperial systems based on Carthage or the Aegean. The establishment of an empire over much of the known world led, though not inevitably, to the provincial maladministration, opportunities for corruption, and the pursuit of personal power which led to economical, political and military collapse. But there remained a vast legacy of culture and science as well as the Grecian traditions which, in some measure Rome had kept as an heirloom.

ROMULUS With Remus the legendary founders of Rome (though the legend is patently of modern manufacture, that is, 4th century B.C., and cast rather clumsily in a Grecian mould). Numitor, last of the Alban kings, had a daughter Rhea Silvia, a vestal virgin, who was made pregnant by Mars. Amulius, the brother of Numitor, had deposed him and ordered the twin boys who were born to Rhea Silvia to be thrown in the Tiber. The mother placed them in a coracle when the river was in flood and Romulus and Remus were washed ashore and suckled by a she-wolf, and later brought up with herdsmen by the king's shepherd Faustulus and his wife Acca Larentia. The twins were natural leaders and they eventually destroyed Amulius and restored Numitor. They built a city for themselves and Romulus walled it, but Remus leapt over the wall and Romulus killed him. The city became a refuge for runaway slaves and runaway homicides, and the inhabitants were provided with wives by inviting the Sabines to a festival and commandeering their women. After ruling over Romans and Sabines for 37 years Romulus died and ascended into heaven as the god Quirinus, a member of the supreme triumvirate which includes Jupiter and Mars.

ROSCIUS (QUINTUS ROSCIUS GALLUS) Roman master of comic acting, born in Latium, the friend of Cicero and Sulla, earned from his art a vast fortune and was officially honoured, died 62 B.C.

ROXANA Daughter of Oxyartes the Bactrian chief, captured by Alexander the Great, captivated him, and they married, 327 B.C. She and their son Alexander Aegus were murdered in Amphipolis, Macedonia by the orders of Cassander in 311 B.C.

RUBICON The stream flowing into the Adriatic a little north of Ariminum (modern Rimini) which marked the southern limit of the territory for which Julius Caesar was responsible as commander in chief of Cisalpine Gaul. He crossed it with his army in 49 B.C., symbolically declaring war on the republic of Rome.

S

SABINA (VIBIA SABINA) Grand-niece of Trajan who became in A.D. 100 the wife of Hadrian, a match made by PLOTINA, whom see. She died in 137, it was said by poisoning or compulsory suicide.

SABINA (POPPAEA SABINA) A beautiful Roman who became the mistress of Nero in A.D. 58, persuaded him to murder his mother Agrippina in 59 and his wife Octavia in 62, after which she married Nero. But in 65 he kicked her while she was pregnant and she died.

SALAMIS An island west of Attica, a naval power until 620 B.C., occupied by the Athenians under Solon, in Macedonian hands from 318 to 232 B.C. The Greeks beat Xerxes of Persia in the great naval battle off the island in 480 B.C.

SALLUST (CAIUS SALLUSTIUS CRISPUS) Roman administrator and historian, 86–34 B.C., born of plebeian stock in Sabine country, entered the administration but was expelled from the Senate in 50 as a supporter of Julius Caesar and as the lover of the wife of Milo, a rowdy politician then in exile for rioting. When Caesar returned to Rome he took him up and in 46 Sallust was appointed governor of Numidia, where he made a large fortune and got off a charge of plundering the province. He bought himself a magnificent estate and wrote seven books of history (of which two survive) before his death in 34 B.C.

SALMONEUS Son of Aeolus, brother of Sisyphus, imitated Zeus

by ordering sacrifices for himself with faked thunder and lightning and was accordingly struck down by a genuine thunderbolt.

SALUS Roman goddess of public health and prosperity.

SAMNIUM A country in central Italy founded by the Samnites, a branch of the Sabines.

SAMOS Politically and culturally important island off the west coast of Asia Minor colonised by Ionians before 1000 B.C., in classic times gradually yielding precedence to Rhodes.

SAMOTHRACE Island in the north Aegean long in naval league with Athens, renowned for its celebration of the mysteries of the CABIRI, which see.

SAPPHO Poet, daughter of Scamandronymus and Cleis, of Eresus and Mytilene in Lesbos, born c. 612 B.C., spent part of her childhood in Sicily but returned to Lesbos and formed a club of young girls devoted to Aphrodite and the Muses, and wrote poems about them and hymns for their marriages. She married Cercylas and had a child Cleis. She resented the tie between her brother Charaxus and the whore RHODOPIS, whom see. She wrote nine books of poems of which little survives, lyrics of tenderness and directness of language, not masking her passion for some of her subjects.

SARDANAPALUS King of Assyria, c. 668–628 B.C., forced back the Ethiopians and conquered Egypt, occupied the realms of Babylon and Arabia, patronised architecture, literature and art.

SARDINIA First colonised by Carthage c. 500 B.C., taken by Rome in 238 and solely exploited as a granary and taxation-field.

SARDIS Fortified capital city of the kingdom of Lydia in Asia Minor, taken by the Persians of Cyrus in 546 B.C., by the Athenians and Ionians in 498, by Antiochus the Great in 215. It was a very early centre of Christianity.

SARPEDON Son of Zeus and Europa, brother of Minos and RHADAMANTHUS, whom see, as a favour from Zeus became king of the Lycians and lived three generations.

SATURNALIA Roman festival in honour of Saturnus, lasting for seven days from 17 December.

SATURNUS A legendary king of Italy identified by the Romans with Cronus and therefore made the father of Jupiter, Neptune, Pluto and Juno, but significantly not of Demeter (the Roman Ceres) most of whose functions in Greek thought are passed over to Saturn. His wife is Ops, the goddess of plenty.

SATYRS (SATYRI) Young goatish rakes of the woods, much addicted to wine and lechery, essential attendants at the worship of Dionysus. More aged members of the species were called Sileni.

SAXONES A tribe which emerged in Germany in the 3rd century A.D. and conquered Britain in the 5th.

SCIPIO The name of a patrician family, from the imperialist point of view the most influential in Rome. Among them, LUCIUS CORNELIUS SCIPIO used the fleet in 259 B.C. to reduce Carthaginian naval bases. CNAEUS CORNELIUS SCIPIO and his brother PUBLIUS fought long campaigns against Hasdrubal in Spain, 217–211 B.C. PUBLIUS CORNELIUS SCIPIO AFRICANUS MAJOR fought at Cannae, defeated Carthage in Spain, and overcame Hannibal in Africa, 216–202, and later fought alongside his brother SCIPIO ASIATICUS in the east, 189.

SCRIBONIA Married as her third husband Octavian (Augustus) in 40 B.C. but was divorced on the day she gave birth to their daughter Julia in 39 so that Octavian could marry Livia. She accompanied JULIA (whom see) into exile in A.D. 2.

SCYLLA 1. The monster dwelling in a cave on the Italian shore of the Fretum Siculum opposite Charybdis. 2. Daughter of king Nisus of Megara who became infatuated with Minos.

SATYR.

SCYROS The Aegean island to which Thetis sent her son Achilles dressed as a girl to avoid his being called to Troy. Here he lay with DEIDAMIA and begot PYRRHUS, whom see.

SCYTHIA The land between the Carpathians and the Don.

SEGESTA (EGESTA, ACESTA) Town in Sicily founded by ACESTES, whom see.

SEJANUS (AELIUS SEJANUS) Commander of the Praetorian Guard of Tiberius who seduced Livilla (see DRUSUS: 2), had Drusus killed, and was plotting to be emperor when he was executed in A.D. 31.

SELENE The goddess of the moon, sister of Helios.

SELEUCIS Syria. SELEUCIA was one of its principal cities. SELEUCUS was the name of a number of its kings.

SEMELE Daughter of Cadmus and Harmonia, was wooed by Zeus and cunningly induced by Hera to request Zeus to appear in the majesty he adopted for his coupling with Hera. He unwillingly appeared as the god of thunder and Semele was killed by his lightning. She was pregnant with Dionysus, whom Zeus preserved and who later retrieved her from the land of Hades. She was deified as Thyone.

SEMIRAMIS Founder with her husband Ninus of the Assyrian empire of Nineveh.

SENECA 1. LUCIUS SENECA, c. 55 B.C. – A.D. 39, Roman rhetorician and literary historian. 2. LUCIUS ANNAEUS SENECA, second son of the preceding, Roman statesman, advocate and philosopher, born in Spain c. 5 B.C., died by forcible suicide A.D. 65 on the discovery of the Pisonian conspiracy against Nero.

SERAPIS Egyptian god adopted by Greece and Rome as the divinity of healing.

SERTORIUS (QUINTUS SERTORIUS) Roman commander,

c. 122–72 B.C., held Spain against Metellus and Pompey for five years but was finally assassinated.

SEVERUS (ALEXANDER SEVERUS) Roman emperor A.D. 222–235.

SEVERUS (FLAVIUS VALERIUS SEVERUS) Roman emperor A.D. 306–307.

SEVERUS (LIBIUS SEVERUS) Roman emperor A.D. 461–465.

SEVERUS (LUCIUS SEPTIMIUS SEVERUS) Roman emperor A.D. 193–211.

SIBYLS (SIBYLLAE) Prophetic women of whom the most famous was to be found at Cumae.

SICILIA Sicily, colonised by the Phoenicians and the Greeks, always in ancient times a fertile granary exporting also wine, honey and fruit, fought for by Carthage and Rome, eventually taken by the Ostrogoths and later a part of the Byzantine empire, A.D. 536–828.

SICYONIA An area in the north-east Peloponnesus.

SIDON The oldest and for long the most powerful city in Phoenicia.

SILENUS A Satyr, son of Hermes, the attendant of Dionysus.

SILURES The tribe occupying South Wales.

SILVANUS Roman god of fields and forests.

SIRENS (SIRENES) Sea-nymphs, seductive in their songs.

SISYPHUS Son of Aeolus, was a king of Corinth whose character was so bad that he was condemned in the lower world to roll up a hill a great block of marble which fell to the bottom as soon as he had got it to the summit.

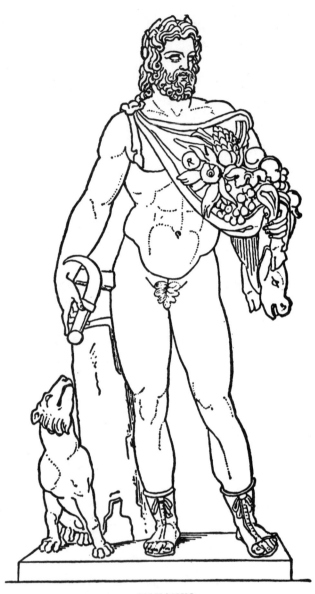

SILVANUS.

SMYRNA Ancient city of west Asia Minor, still flourishing.

SOCRATES Athenian philosopher, 469–399 B.C., husband of Xanthippe who was later said to have been a shrew, devoted himself to enquiry through his question-and-answer dialogue into the proper conduct of life, was tried in 399 for corrupting youth and introducing strange gods and, unable to convince his judges that he was not a subversive character, duly drank the prescribed hemlock. He personifies the eternal enquiry into the truths of moral philosophy and a cool scientific respect for logic.

SOLON Athenian lawgiver, c. 635–560 B.C., reformed the constitution on a democratic basis.

SOMNUS The Roman version of Hypnos, god of sleep, the brother of Death.

SOPHOCLES Tragic playwright born at Colonus, Athens c. 496 B.C., began his fame as a performer, being a handsome leader of public dancing and performer of music on the lyre. As a dramatist he challenged Aeschylus and was awarded the prize in the contest, upon which Aeschylus left Athens for Sicily. Later Euripides in turn challenged Sophocles. In his old age his son Iophon tried to gain control of his property on the grounds of his senility, but the case was thrown out after a dramatically virile speech by Sophocles. Seven of his alleged 130 plays survive.

SOPHISTS Popular educators practising in Athens in the 5th century B.C.

SOPHONISBA The daughter of Hasdrubal of Carthage, betrothed to MASINISSA, whom see, but later given in a dynastic marriage to a rival king of Numidia, Syphax, whom Masinissa defeated. Masinissa fell in love with Sophonisba and married her, but Scipio Africanus would not ratify the union and demanded the surrender of Sophonisba. Masinissa sent in to his wife a bowl of poison which she drank rather than go into captivity.

SPARTA (LACEDAEMON) Capital of Laconia and chief city of the Peloponnesus, after much dissension was given a viable constitution by

Lycurgus and began the territorial expansion which through the centuries matched it against Athens, Macedon and Rome.

SPARTACUS A Thracian soldier who deserted in order to lead a force of bandits and was captured and sold to be a gladiator in the circus at Rome. While under training in Capua in 73 B.C. he and some seventy others broke out of barracks and took cover in the crater of Vesuvius. The band of dissidents attracted great numbers of runaway slaves and displaced persons, particularly after Spartacus and his band had cut their way through a force of 3000 soldiers which threatened to trap them. A number of other victories, and the booty that went with them, eventually swelled the army controlled by Spartacus to 90,000 men who gradually fought their way north to the Alps. Here Spartacus had hoped they would disperse to make the journey to their original homes, but their continued success had changed their mood and to remain as an established army seemed their best mode of existence. Spartacus turned south and ravaged Italy for the second time. After two years and many military victories he was defeated by Marcus Licinius Crassus in 71 B.C. in a battle where Spartacus was killed and his survivors were mainly crucified.

SPES (to the Greeks ELPIS) The goddess of hope, personified in sculpture in Greece but allocated a number of temples in Rome.

SPHINX In the Greek conception the monstrous daughter of TYPHON (whom see) and Echidna or Chimaera, a winged lion with a woman's breast and head. In Egypt the figure had no wings. The Sphinx demanded human sacrifice from the Thebans every time her riddle concerning the three ages of man was unanswered. Oedipus answered it and she killed herself.

SPORADES The group of scattered islands in the Aegean between Crete and Asia Minor.

STABIAE The coast town where the elder Pliny died during the eruption of Vesuvius, A.D. 79: modern Castellammare di Stabia.

STATIUS (PUBLIUS PAPINIUS STATIUS) Roman poet,

SIREN.

native of Naples, renowned both for epic and extempore verse, A.D. 45–96.

STENTOR The Greek herald in the Trojan war whose voice was as loud as fifty others together.

STHENELUS 1. Father of Cycnus, the youth changed into a swan. 2. A tragic playwright attacked by Aristophanes.

STILICHO A general of the emperor Theodosius I who was virtual ruler of the western empire under his successor Honorius. The patron of Claudian, killed at Ravenna in A.D. 408.

STOICS The school of philosophers founded by Zeno in his lectures in the Stoa Poikile, a public hall in Athens, from about 300 B.C. Emphasising the supremacy of duty, it clearly opposed epicureanism.

STRABO A Greek historian and geographer born in Pontus, 64 B.C. – A.D. 21. About a quarter of his known work survives.

STYX The Nymph, daughter of Oceanus and Tethys, who gave her name to the river which flows in seven concentric circles round the underworld. Because of the help she gave Zeus in his war against the Titans Zeus made an oath by Styx, a cup of the water of Styx being poured as the oath was spoken, the most solemn and binding undertaking which a god could make.

SUADA (To the Greeks, PITHO) The personification of persuasion.

SUETONIUS (TRANQUILLUS SUETONIUS) Roman historian, c. A.D. 69–140, friend of the younger Pliny and at one time secretary to Hadrian, wrote the extant Lives of the Caesars.

SULLA (LUCIUS CORNELIUS SULLA) Roman dictator, born 138 B.C., whose steady military successes and personal antipathy to Marius gained him the consulship in 88 B.C. as the choice of the aristocratic party in Rome. This appointment gained him the command of the army to be sent to fight Mithridates. Marius challenged it and got a vote conferring the command upon himself. Sulla marched with his army on Rome and expelled Marius, then fought a successful campaign in Greece, sacked Athens, and re-instated Mithridates in a questionable policy decision. In 83 he returned to Italy and there was civil war for a year, after which Sulla was undisputed master of Italy, dictator in Rome (from 81), a cruelly oppressive though administratively reforming autocrat, the precursor of the later dictatorship of the Caesars. He resigned office in 79 and died the next year.

SUNIUM A headland on the southernmost tip of Attica and the name of the town there which maintained a temple to Athena, still visible in part.

SYMPLEGADES Two islands at the entrace to the Hellespont, known as the Clashing Rocks because they moved to squeeze in ships that passed between them. The Argo was miraculously sailed through and the rocks then became fixed.

SYMPOSIUM Formally a drinking party, in fact a *salon* with a varying amount of entertainment but constant discussion and conversation.

SYPHAX King of a tribe of the Numidians, died 203 B.C., for whom see MASINISSA, SOPHONISBA.

SYRACUSAE The most thriving town in Sicily, having the advantage of two splendid harbours; founded from Corinth in 734 B.C., after civil upheaval became a tyranny under Gelon, 485 and Hieron, died 467, after which a new democracy showed its strength by twice resisting Athenian invasion, 424 and 413. But danger from the ambitions of Carthage encouraged the acceptance of DIONYSUS as tyrant, whom see, in 406. From the third century B.C. the city was a shuttlecock in the struggle between Rome and Carthage, and by 212 B.C. it was a part of Roman Sicily.

SYRIA The country between the Mediterranean and the Tigris.

SYRINX A Nymph of Arcadia who escaped from pursuit by Pan through being changed into a reed, through which Pan piped.

SYRTES Two dangerous gulfs off north Africa: Syrtis Major, dangerous for its sandbanks, Syrtis Minor for its shelving rocky shore, uncertain tide depths and frequent onshore winds.

T

TACITUS (CORNELIUS TACITUS) Roman historian born *c.*
A.D. 55, married the daughter of Agricola in 77, beyond which little is
known of his life save that he was a friend and colleague of the younger
Pliny and was proconsul in Asia about 112 and died after 115. He wrote
the life of his father-in-law Agricola in 98 and two main works covering
the history of Rome between A.D. 14 and 98, not all of which survives.

TAENARUM A headland in Laconia where a temple to Poseidon
offered absolute sanctuary. Through a cave in the cliff Heracles dragged
Cerberus into the upper world, and a statue on the shore commemorated
the spot as the place where Arion was brought ashore on a dolphin.
(Modern Cape Matapan.)

TALASSIO (To the Greeks, HYMENAEUS) Roman god of
marriage.

TANAIS The river Don.

TANTALUS Son of Zeus and a nymph called Pluto, a vaguely-
defined earth-deity, he was a wealthy king of Aipylos in Lydia, was the
father of Niobe and of PELOPS, whom see for the disgusting meal
offered to the gods by Tantalus. His punishment was to stand for ever in a
lak e in Tartarus with a fruit tree over his head, but both water and fruit
rec eded when he reached for it, and in addition a huge stone poised over
his head put him in constant fear.

TANTALUS, SISYPHUS, IXION.

TARENTUM Modern Taranto, a Greek trading point in southern Italy from 1200 B.C. and a Spartan settlement from 708 B.C., became the most powerful city in Magna Graecia but, falling to the Romans after the wars involving Pyrrhus, 275 B.C., and Hannibal, 209 B.C., it was wilfully run down in importance to the advantage of Brundisium, modern Brindisi.

TARPEIAN ROCK The cliff on the Capitoline Hill, from which criminals and traitors were thrown, in Rome.

TARQUINIUS The family which traditionally provided TAR-QUINIUS PRISCUS, the fifth king of Rome, 616–579 B.C. and TARQUINIUS SUPERBUS, 534–510 B.C., the last king of Rome, for whose expulsion see LUCRETIA.

TARSUS The principal city of Cilicia.

TARTARUS Son of Aether and Ge, and by union with Ge the father of the Gigantes, Typhoeus and Echidna, later ruled over a gated territory as far below the lands of Hades as heaven is above the earth.

TELAMON Brother of PELEUS, whom see, became king of Salamis and father of Ajax, was one of the Calydonian hunters and a friend of Heracles.

TELEGONUS The son of Odysseus and Circe.

TELEMACHUS The son of Odysseus and Penelope.

TELEPHUS The son of Heracles and Auge, became king of Mysia and was important in the literary plot of the *Iliad*.

TELLUS The Roman Mother Earth, goddess of fertility.

TEMPE An idyllically situated valley in Thessaly.

TENEDOS A small island in the Aegean off Troy.

[205]

TEREUS The deceitful husband of Procne and ravisher of PHILO-MELA, whom see.

TERMINUS The Roman god of boundaries. His milestones and boundary-stones became occasional altars.

TERPANDER Greek musician and poet of the 7th century B.C., a pioneer of lyric poetry.

TERPSICHORE The Muse of choral song and dancing.

TETHYS Daughter of Uranus and Ge, wife of Oceanus, mother of the Oceanides.

TEUCER 1. The first king of Troy. 2. Son of TELAMON, whom see, the most skilful archer among the Greeks at Troy.

TEUTONES North Germans who invaded Gaul in the 2nd century B.C.

THAIS Athenian courtesan taken by Alexander the Great into Asia and passed on to Ptolemy Lagi on Alexander's death.

THALES Mathematician of Miletus who was famous for having accurately predicted a tactically important eclipse of the sun on 28 May 585 B.C.

THALIA 1. The Muse of comedy. 2. One of the Graces.

THANATOS (To the Romans, MORS) The god of death.

THARGELIA The annual festival to Apollo in Athens.

THEBAE (THEBES) 1. The principal city in Boeotia. 2. The principal city of Egypt until the rise of Alexandria.

THEMIS Daughter of Uranus and Ge, though originally identified with Ge or Mother Earth, the second-ranking wife of Zeus and by him

THEMIS.

the mother of The Morai (Fates), the Horae (Seasons) and Irene. She personifies the virtues of regularity and good order.

THEMISTOCLES Athenian statesman, *c.* 528–462 B.C., the political leader of Athens from 489, partly through having his opponents ostracised, committed Athenian prosperity to maritime commerce and power which was justified by the Greek victory over the Persians at Salamis. He later committed himself to personal intrigue in the conflict between Athens and Sparta, was denounced and fled for his life to Persia, where he died.

THEOCRITUS Bucolic poet from Syracuse, *fl. c.* 275 B.C.

THEODORICUS (THEODORIC) 1. King of the Visigoths from A.D. 418–451. 2. THEODORIC THE GREAT, king of the Ostrogoths, conquered Italy and ruled it A.D. 493–526.

THEODOSIUS 1. THEODOSIUS THE GREAT, Roman emperor of the east from A.D. 379, but by settling the problem of the Goths there and elsewhere re-established the unity of the west. A Christian of strict orthodoxy, his massacre of the population of Thessalonica in the circus amphitheatre as a reprisal for the murder of a platoon of troops provoked St. Ambrose, bishop of Milan to refuse him entry into the cathedral until he had done public penance. He died in Milan in 395. 2. THEODOSIUS II, emperor A.D. 408–450.

THEOPHRASTUS Greek philosopher, *c.* 370–288 B.C., the favourite pupil of Aristotle, and his successor in the presidency of the Lyceum. ´

THEOPOMPUS Greek historian born *c.* 378 B.C., a native of Chios who had to flee the country in his old age.

THERMOPYLAE The pass leading from Thessaly to Locris defended by the Spartans against Xerxes in 480 B.C.

THERON Tyrant of Agrigentum (Acragas) 488–472 B.C., father-in-law of Gelon and victor with him of the battle against the Carthaginians at Himera, 480. He was a friend of Pindar, a great force for culture and he notably beautified his city.

THERSITES An aggressive cripple among the Greeks at Troy, killed by Achilles for ridiculing his grief for PENTHESILEA, whom see.

THESEUS The great legendary hero of Athens, son of Aegeus or Poseidon, in his youth did almost as many feats of valour as Heracles, slew the Minotaur, sailed from Crete with Ariadne, became king of Athens, fought the war against the Amazons and figured in many of the heroic expeditions of legend.

THESPIS The Greek playwright who, by introducing an actor to relieve the chorus (wearing different masks on different occasions) has been called the father of Greek tragedy. He is known to have won a prize in 534 B.C.

THESSALONICA A city in Macedonia enlarged by Cassander in 315 B.C. and called after his wife, the sister of Alexander the Great. Modern Salonkia.

THESSALY (THESSALIA) The largest natural area of Greece, north of the Epirus.

THETIS Daughter of Nereus and Doris, a sea-goddess more notable than other Nereids with some of the gifts of PROTEUS, whom see. She was married against her will to Peleus and became the mother of Achilles.

THISBE A Babylonian Juliet, not allowed by her parents to marry her lover Pyramus, with whom she could only converse through a crack in the wall separating their houses. They arranged a rendezvous at Ninus' tomb. Thisbe arrived first and fled from a lioness which had just attacked an ox. She dropped her cloak which the animal soiled with blood. Pyramus found the cloak, thought the worst, and killed himself under a mulberry tree. Thisbe came back and did the same.

THRACE (THRACIA) The eastern part of the Balkans, peopled from 1300 B.C. by savage cannibals who, however, passed on to the Greeks important elements of religion, poetry and music. The Greeks later traded with them and Macedonia enlisted their men as mercenaries, but it

THESEUS AND THE MINOTAUR.

remained a warring, anarchic territory until the Romans stamped it into some shape from about 12 B.C.

THUCYDIDES Athenian historian and general, *c.* 455–400 B.C., drew his fortune from gold mines in Thrace, failed in his military career, wrote a most highly regarded history of the war between Athens and Sparta 431–404 B.C. which does not survive in full.

THULE Traditionally the last island in the north of the world, six days' sail from Britain. Agricola's fleet, saying that they had sighted it, referred to it as Shetland.

THURII Greek town in Lucania where Herodotus was born.

THYONE The name of Semele after she had been retrieved from the land of Hades by Dionysus, and deified.

THYRSUS The wand carried by Dionysus and those who celebrated his worship.

TIBER (TIBRIS, TIBERINUS) The riber Tiber, modern Tevere.

TIBERIUS (TIBERIUS JULIUS CAESAR AUGUSTUS) Roman emperor, born 42 B.C., the son of Tiberius Claudius Nero and Livia, the latter being divorced in 38 to marry Augustus. He served as a professional soldier until he was over fifty years old. In 12 B.C. he was compelled to divorce Vipsania Agrippina and marry Julia, widow of Agrippa and daughter of Augustus, an unhappy union which, allied with Tiberius' uncertain temper, caused him to retire to Rhodes for eight years in 6 B.C. Circumstances forced Augustus to acknowledge him as heir presumptive, and he was emperor from A.D. 14 until his death at Capraca (modern Capri) in A.D. 37, being smothered there by members of the Praetorian Guard after ten years of alleged debauchery on the island.

TIBULLUS (ALBIUS TIBULLUS) Roman elegiac poet *c.* 48–19 B.C.

TIBUR A resort in the hills 16 miles north-east of Rome, modern Tivoli.

TIMAEUS Rhetorician of Tauromenius, Sicily, *c.* 356–260 B.C., who was exiled to Athens and wrote a valuable history of Sicily.

TIMANTHES Greek painter of Sicyon, late 5th century B.C.

TIMON 1. Legendary Athenian misanthrope. 2. Athenian lampoonist *c.* 320–230 B.C.

TIMOTHEUS Athenian dithyrambic poet from Miletus, *c.* 450–360 B.C.

TINGIS (TINGI) Modern Tangier.

TIRESIAS Legendary blind soothsayer of Thebes, said to have been blinded for a number of reasons, one being that he had decided a dispute between Zeus and Hera in favour of Hera, who said that women got more pleasure from love than men.

TIRYNS A town in Argolis where Heracles was brought up.

TITANS (TITANES) The children of Heaven and Earth (Uranus and Ge) who allied themselves with Cronus but were defeated by his son Zeus: named as Oceanus, Coeus, Crius, Hyperion, Iapetus, Theia, Rhea, Themis, Mnemosyne, Phoebe, Tethys, Cronus.

TITHONUS Brother of Priam who was granted by Eos immortality but not eternal youth, so that he lived as a shrunken old man.

TITUS (TITUS FLAVIUS VESPIANUS) Roman emperor A.D. 79–81, the son of Vespasian, born A.D. 39, served as a general in Britain, Germany and Judaea, besieged and sacked Jerusalem in 70, in Rome completed the Colosseum.

TOMIS Modern Costanza, where Ovid died in exile.

TRAJAN (MARCUS ULPIUS TRAIANUS) Roman emperor A.D. 98–117, born near Seville probably A.D. 52, professional soldier, consul in 91 and frequently afterwards, pacified Dacia and Parthia 98–103, conquered Parthia 115–116, proved himself a good imperial administrator.

TRIPTOLEMUS.

TRITONS.

TRASIMENE (LACUS TRASIMENUS) The lake in Etruria near which Hannibal beat Flaminius 217 B.C.

TREBONIUS (CAIUS TREBONIUS) In 55 B.C. as tribune of the plebs put through the *Lex Trebonia* conferring territorial commands on Pompey, Crassus and Caesar, consul in 45 B.C., conspired for the murder of Caesar in 44, assassinated by Dolabella in 43.

TRIPTOLEMUS Son of Celeus king of Eleusis, a protégé of Demeter, invented the plough and became a hero of the Eleusinian mysteries.

TRITON Son of Poseidon and Amphitrite, a fish-tailed god of the sea represented as blowing on a conch as his 'wreathed horn'.

TROILUS Son of Priam (or Apollo) and Hecuba, killed at Troy by Achilles.

TROS Father of Ilus, king of Phrygia, gave his name to Troy.

TROY The city on which the Trojan war was centred, four miles east of the Dardanelles.

TULLIUS 1. TULLIUS HOSTILIUS, third king of Rome. 2. SERVIUS TULLIUS, sixth king of Rome.

TURNUS King of the Rutili betrothed to Lavinia who fought Aeneas on her account and was killed by him.

TYCHE (To the Romans FORTUNA) The goddess of fortune.

TYDEUS Son of Oenus king of Calydon, father of Diomedes, killed at Thebes and deliberately not immortalised by Athena though she had previously promised this.

TYPHON (TYPHOEUS) A hundred-headed monster subdued by Zeus with a thunderbolt and buried under Aetna.

TYRE (TYRUS) A magnificent city of Phoenicia.

UV

ULYSSES See ODYSSEUS.

UMBRIA The district in Italy south of the Rubicon and bordering the Adriatic.

URANIA A Muse, daughter of Zeus and Mnemosyne, consecrated to astronomy.

UTICA Phoenician colony in north Africa which inherited most of the territory of Carthage after the third Punic war.

VALENS Emperor of the east A.D. 364–378.

VALENTIANUS 1. Roman emperor A.D. 364–375. 2. Roman emperor A.D. 375–392. 3. Roman emperor A.D. 425–455.

VALERIANUS (PUBLICIUS LICINIUS VALERIANUS) Roman emperor A.D. 253–260, died as a greatly maltreated prisoner of the Persians.

VALERIUS MAXIMUS (VALERIUS ANTIAS) Author of wholly unreliable series of historical anecdotes in the early 1st century A.D.

VANDALS (VANDALI) A Germanic confederacy originating on the

Baltic, very active depredators in the 5th and 6th centuries A.D., sacked
Rome A.D. 455.

VARRO 1. CAIUS TERENTIUS VARRO, consul defeated by
Hannibal at Cannae 216 B.C., later a distinguished statesman. 2.
MARCUS TERENTIUS VARRO, 116–27 B.C., a prolific writer
on grammar, agriculture, philosophy and general knowledge, said to have
written 490 books.

VARUS (PUBLIUS QUINCTILIUS VARUS) Famous as the
commander who lost his entire army in an attack by Arminius of Germany
in A.D. 9.

VENUS Originally an Italian, not Roman, goddess of Spring, later
identified with Aphrodite.

VERCINGETORIX Acclaimed king of the Arverni tribe after his
successful revolt against Caesar in Gaul in 52 B.C., defeated in 46 and killed
in Rome after being displayed in Caesar's triumph.

VERRES (CAIUS VERRES) Plundering governor of Sicily 73–70
B.C. prosecuted by Cicero and sent into exile.

VESPASIAN (TITUS FLAVIUS SABINUS VESPASIANUS)
Roman emperor A.D. 69–79, born A.D. 9, served as a general in Britain
A.D. 43 and subdued the Isle of Wight, conducted the war against the
Jews from A.D. 66, was proclaimed emperor at Alexandria and ruled
modestly and well.

VESTA The Roman goddess of the hearth, regarded as the centre of the
home, so that in effect she had an altar in every house besides the great
sanctuary in the Forum attended by the Vestal Virgins.

VESUVIUS Volcano, the first great recorded eruption of which over-
whelmed Pompeii and Herculaneum on 24 August A.D. 79.

VIPSANIA AGRIPPINA The wife of Tiberius, forcibly divorced on the orders of Augustus in 12 B.C. so that he could marry Julia, daughter of Augustus.

VIRGIL (PUBLIUS VERGILIUS MARO) Roman poet born near Mantua in 70 B.C., educated at Cremona, Milan and Rome as a rhetorician, physician and astronomer, but changed to the study of philosophy and the writing of poetry, became intimate with Maecenas and Horace, immediately famous for the *Georgics* and the *Aeneid*, died 19 B.C.

VIRTUS The Roman personification of manly valour, represented as a victorious armed virgin.

VITELLIUS (AULUS VITELLIUS) An unmajestic and unmilitary glutton born A.D. 15, proclaimed emperor by his soldiers at Cologne and ruled through the twelve months of A.D. 69 before being beaten to death and thrown down the GEMONIAE steps, which see.

VOLSCI Native tribe of central Italy not entirely subdued by the Romans until 338 B.C. See CORIOLANUS.

VULCAN (VULCANUS) The Roman god of fire, of equal antiquity as Vesta, but finally identified as Hephaestus.

VESTAL VIRGIN.

HEROES OF THE TROJAN WAR.

XZ

XANTHIPPE The wife of SOCRATES, whom see.

XANTHUS 1. The most prominent city of Lycia. 2. A writer from Lydia, 5th century B.C., recording folk-myths.

XENOCRATES Philosopher, disciple of Plato, and president of the Academy 339–314 B.C.

XENOPHANES A philosopher and poet from Colophon who lived for 67 years of his long life in Sicily, late 6th century B.C.

XENOPHON Athenian general who marched under Cyrus against Artaxerxes in 401 B.C., conducted the army's retreat into Thrace but was shortly afterwards banished from Athens, fought for Sparta and subsequently retired to Corinth, probably dying in 354 B.C. He wrote a history of the campaign of Cyrus and a continuation of the work of Thucydides.

XERXES Succeeded Darius I as king of Persia in 485 B.C. and inherited the task of overcoming the Greek alliance, which had supported the revolt of the Ionian Greek colonies in Asia Minor and, when challenged, had defeated the Persians at Marathon in 490. After some time taken up in subduing revolts in Egypt, Xerxes moved against the Greeks in 480, crossing the Hellespont on a bridge of boats and digging a canal across the isthmus of Athos for the better security of his fleet. He marched through Macedonia and Thessaly, finally overcame the Greek stand at Thermopylae, and entered Athens as his fleet sailed into Phalerum Bay. This fleet was defeated by the Greeks at Salamis, and Xerxes retreated in the same year all the way to Sardis in Lydia, whence he had started. He left in Greece forces under his general Mardonius, who was decisively beaten at Plataea in the next year, 479. Little more is known of Xerxes except that he was murdered by Artabanus in a palace revolt in 465 B.C.

ZAMA REGIA A town in Numidia, north Africa which may have been the site of the battle of Zama in 202 B.C., when Scipio Africanus defeated Hannibal and brought the second Punic war to an end.

ZELA A town in Pontus near which Mithridates VI defeated the Roman general Triarius in 67 B.C. and Julius Caesar defeated Pharnaces II, son of Mithridates, in 47, afterwards sending to Rome the famous despatch: *Veni, vidi, vici.*

ZENO Phoenician philosopher, 335–263 B.C., working in Athens from 313, where he founded the STOIC school of philosophy, which see.

ZENOBIA The beautiful and ruthless queen of Palmyra in Syria who in A.D. 267 murdered her husband Odaenathus, who had been given wide kingly powers by the Romans, and set out to become Queen of the East, conquering Egypt and much of Asia Minor. She was defeated at Palmyra in 273 and taken to Rome for Aurelian's triumph in 274, after which she was pensioned off in a villa at Tibur.

ZEPHYRUS The west wind, the son of Astraeus the Titan and Eos goddess of dawn, the parents of all winds and stars.

ZEUS Became for the Greeks, from Indo-European origin, their principal god by his defeat of his father CRONUS (whom see). Of the sons of Cronus Hades took the lower world, Poseidon the sea, and Zeus the heavens and upper regions of the earth including mountain tops. The surface of the earth was common ground. His sanctions were thunder and lightning, occasionally used in a somewhat petty way in the course of pursuing, or concealing, various seductions on which he had determined to the chagrin of his wife Hera. But he could also assume a role of awesome majesty. For the birth and boyhood of Zeus see RHEA.

[222]

THE MARRIAGE OF ZEUS AND HERA.

ZEUXIS A painter who came to Athens from his birthplace in Heraclea, southern Italy in about 430 B.C., was a skilful initiator of high-lighting and gradations of colour-shading, and is famous for one bunch of grapes he painted which a bird tried to eat.

ZOROASTER The founder of the Magian religion among the Persians, possibly around 800 B.C.